About the author

During 28 years as a Consultant Physician in Plymouth Hospital Alec Forbes became increasingly aware of the psychological and nutritional causes of disease, as well as the old and new approaches to health care. In 1977 he became a healer member of the National Federation of Spiritual Healers. Two years later the World Health Organisation appointed him advisor to its Traditional Medicine Programme. He left the NHS in 1980 to develop a working example of a new medical model for wholistic health care.

THE BRISTOL DIET

A Get Well and Stay Well Eating Plan

Dr Alec Forbes MA, DM, FRCP

**CENTURY PUBLISHING
LONDON**

FOR NORAH – THANKS

Copyright © Dr Alec Forbes 1984

All rights reserved
First published in Great Britain in 1984
by Century Publishing Co. Ltd,
Portland House,
12–13 Greek Street, London W1V 5LE.

Reprinted 1984 (*three times*), 1985

ISBN 0 7126 0326 3

Photoset by Rowland Phototypesetting Ltd,
Bury St Edmunds, Suffolk
Printed and bound in Great Britain in 1985
by Richard Clay Ltd, Bungay, Suffolk.

CONTENTS

PREFACE

My interest in diet began in 1937 when I first went up to Magdalen College, Oxford, and found that Dr Hugh Sinclair was my tutor. Hugh is probably the most original, possibly the greatest, living dietetic scientist. In addition to pointing my interests in this direction, he taught me that we should never take anything for granted and to be open to every alternative explanation for a given set of facts.

Hugh's teachings were very much to my taste, and although it was hard to keep up with him at the time, I worked these ideas out later in my professional life and studied diets world-wide among the many therapies that actually outnumber orthodox or, more accurately, allopathic medicine.

In fact two-thirds of the world uses systems other than the allopathic. I have looked at vegetarian, Hindu, Chinese and Japanese diets, because these systems use carefully worked out ways of changing diet in order to correct emotional and physical illnesses. In the Western culture, naturopathic diets are equivalents of Eastern practices which can be called vitalistic as opposed to mechanistic, chemical or technological.

I tested out these diets first by eating them myself and then by applying them to my patients.

The diet I arrived at has been used for about ten years in guiding those patients of mine who would accept such ideas. Because it took too long to explain, I had a short version of this diet printed and used to sell it to them. This was well received and was about to go into its third edition, when I had an offer I could not refuse and took early retirement from the National Health Service to help in setting up the Cancer Help Centre in Bristol. The diet was then adapted for use by cancer patients, but it is applicable to all conditions and to the prevention of disease.

pee
cho
wa
O
hire
wh

1
HOW TO
USE THE BOOK

Most people who need to follow a diet just want simple instructions that tell them exactly what they must eat. They don't want to know the whys and wherefores of what they are eating. On the other hand, there are those people who like to pick things over carefully and know exactly why they are doing what they are asked to do. It is hard to satisfy the demands of such people in a book of this size. But everything in this diet fits in with all the systems of medicine that I have studied and with recent advances in nutritional science. The diet may not satisfy all the vitalistic practitioners of naturopathy, Ayurvedic medicine, Chinese medicine and Japanese macrobiotic medicine, nor all allopathic medical practitioners, because it is a marriage of many systems – and no marriage is successful unless there is continuous give and take between the partners.

Chapters 1, 2, 3, 6, 7 and 8, and Appendix 1 are for the first group of people – those who just want instructions. Chapters 6 and 8, and Appendix 1 are the basic minimum. Photostat these and make a small pamphlet from them, if you wish, for quick reference in the kitchen. The rest of the book is about the whys and the wherefores of the diet.

The Get Well Diet, described in Chapter 6, is quite a tough cleansing process, because it helps you get rid of junk from the inside while at the same time providing minerals and vitamins necessary for restoring the proper functioning of the body. It takes about a month to change over from normal eating habits and, once you are fully on the diet, it should be maintained for a further eight weeks.

The work of the Get Well Diet could be done by juice fasting in six weeks or less if you were able to start the diet immediately. But most Western people fight shy of this approach, which is why the diet is a 'solid juice fast'.

After three months it is necessary to ask yourself whether you are one of the third of the average Western population bred on a mixed meat and vegetable diet who ought to be vegetarian. You will know if you are one of these because you will feel so much better than you have ever felt in your life before, and won't want to go back to what you used to eat. However, if you still crave some meat this may be because you do need it. Perhaps you cannot produce the enzymes which convert vegetable protein into human protein and you should resume eating some fish, free-range chicken and eggs.

If you have cancer, you should not go back to red meat. It contains a lot of growth hormones. Make sure that the chickens you do eat have not been filled up with hormones to caponise and fatten them.

The follow-up diet is the Stay Well Diet. It contains about 50 per cent raw vegetable food and a lot more cooked food, and in fact you will see from the list given in Appendix 1 that there is a wide range of foods from which you can select your meals. You should have no difficulty in finding something you like, though you may have to change your eating habits a little.

Many people who are vegetarian for emotional reasons will disagree with me when I say that only one-third of the adult population of the Western countries can become strictly vegan, i.e. taking no milk, no eggs, no butter and nothing made with animal products. Of course, we could breed people selectively to be 100 per cent vegan without much difficulty in probably two or three generations. The Brahmins and the Buddhists in several countries are entirely vegetarian and remain in perfectly good health. They have been bred selectively for many generations to be vegans.

I was a vegetarian for a long time and know that I took a nutritionally correct diet, but after seven years I was getting very weak muscularly and was also quite thin because my muscles were wasting. At first I thought that I was suffering from motor neurone disease, which afflicts the elderly and is incurable, so I did not do much about it. Then I heard of the work of Dr Kelly in the United States and his classification of various dietary types of people, some of whom can eat only vegetables and remain in good health and some of whom need quite a lot of meat to stay well. I went to visit him, looked at his work and thought that it was on the right lines.

Then I remembered how much better I used to feel when I went on holiday in the Greek Islands, where I found I could swim much further than usual and felt very vigorous. It is almost impossible to get a decent vegetarian diet there, so I did eat meat. When I came home my new strength soon fell away again when I went back to a strict vegetarian diet. So I started gradually to eat meat, eggs and fish in small amounts, without putting on any more fat, which I could measure by the thickness of the rolls on my tummy, my weight went up and so did muscular bulk and power and ability to swim longer and longer distances. I can now swim two miles – a mile at a time there and back – non-stop. This is more than I have ever done in my life, so I think there is something in this theory that not everybody can be vegetarian.

This situation has probably come about because many people have had the ability to transform vegetable proteins into human protein bred out of their bodies, or they have lost this ability because they have been fed on meat from childhood. Therefore they are now dependent upon animals who are able to transform food for them. They have lost, and cannot remake, the necessary enzymes.

The position could be changed by trying all children on a vegetarian diet from birth. Many would adapt to this; children are more adaptable than adults. Gradually a race of healthy, ecologically harmonious vegetarians would evolve. This may surprise the meat eaters but, speaking as one who has been both a meat eater and a vegetarian, I am sure that I am more peaceful and feel cleaner and sharper when I eat a lot of vegetables.

At first glance, the menus look as though they are low on protein. This is because we get used to taking our food from animal sources and we eat much more protein than is needed. We do not know, or have forgotten, that many vegetables contain large amounts of protein, and if they are carefully selected and mixed as indicated in Chs 4, 6 and 7 we need never be short of protein. In fact people in the West tend to make a fetish of eating meat and maintaining a high protein diet. This type of diet can, of course, help to reduce weight, but it has some disadvantages. It may give you a high blood pressure and also cancer, because your fat intake is high if you eat meat.

The meat we eat today is carefully bred, fed and treated with female sex hormones to make it very fat. It is not the lean meat of an animal that lives free and has to be caught before it can be eaten. During the last 30 years I have noticed that younger men are developing bigger breasts. It seems possible that this may be due to their increased intake of female sex hormones. Their meat intake has certainly increased.

The length of our intestinal tract is about 32 feet which indicates that we evolved as vegetable eaters. The intestinal tract of a meat-eating animal of similar size is about 6–8 feet in length. Because of this, the meat is only partially digested and passes out of the animal before it has a chance to putrefy and break down into irritating products of fermentation. It was probably a sudden drastic change in climate that forced people into meat eating; certainly killing to eat would have been less troublesome and time-consuming than tilling the soil. Today the meat-rearing business uses up about seven to nine times more land than vegetable growing would if we ate only vegetables. And animals are poor converters of protein. Their efficiency in this is only 30 per cent.

It may surprise some people to know that if the soya bean is treated as it is by the Japanese, a cheesy substance called tofu is produced, containing up to 40 per cent protein. This is higher than the protein content of meat, which varies between 25–30 per cent.

The Bristol Diet was not originally intended for cancer patients; it was intended to help in the prevention of all disease and to encourage a positive attitude towards good health. At the Cancer Help Centre we find that patients say, 'Oh, I've lost my rheumatism' or 'My piles don't trouble me any more' or 'My asthma is better' or 'My rash has gone.' The same applies to their relatives who often share the diet. They too improve in health. One lady described how she had resigned herself to middle-age aches, swollen ankles and thick legs, but how after six months of the diet her asthma and migraine had disappeared, her legs were slim and she could walk up hills, well, almost as fast as her son who was our patient.

So, although the Bristol Diet has been carefully based upon the raw vegetable diet that many people in recent times have used to cure themselves of cancer, it is also useful for many other conditions, and will help everyone to enjoy a healthier life.

2
FOOD – WHAT IT IS AND HOW TO MANAGE IT

Some people say that 'you are what you eat'. But it is not as simple as that. You are what you eat, what you can digest, what you can absorb and what you can metabolise – that is, use chemically in your body. But there is no doubt that what we eat and how we live are the two main causes of disease. It is hard to alter the situation outside our bodies, but the food we take in and how we think, feel and relate to others is within our control. The question we must answer is do we really want to take charge of ourselves, or are we so bound by the habits of eating, thinking and feeling that we are just automatic machines running along fixed paths assuming that we are and will continue to be all right?

When I was in practice in Plymouth, it was quite common for me to have to say to a patient, 'Look – if you don't change your eating habits or way of life, you'll always be ill with this particular problem and will have to take drugs to keep you comfortable for the rest of your life.' Generally, after a short pause for thought, the answer was, 'Give me the pills.'

We live in a world that is always changing and this is also true of dietary and social habits. As these change so our diseases change. We believe that everything is getting better and better, yet no sooner have we got over one set of disease problems – take the infective diseases, for example – than other chronic diseases start to become more common. These then spread back into younger age groups. In fact we do not live very much longer than our ancestors did and the total amount of sickness, that is ill-health and sub-health, remains about the same. In the current pattern of health the incidence of bacterial infection is far lower than that of chronic sickness affecting the middle-aged – mainly mental, arterial, cancer, more virus infections and auto-immune disease. Therefore, while we have the illusion of progress, nothing really changes and unless we do something pretty quickly about the flood of pollution that is bursting over us, we will be even sicker as a result of the way that we live now.

A hundred and fifty years ago there were many bacterial infections and chronic diseases that affected mainly the young and the old. People ate a great deal of wholegrain bread, their fat consumption was small and sugar consumption was negligible. In those days only the rich ate a lot of meat and sugar. We now eat enormous amounts of sugar, fat and meat. Bread and flour intake is about a third of what it was and still falling. Moreover, it is mostly white, or white flour coloured brown.

Two major killing diseases in the West today are hardening of the arteries (atheroma) and cancer. It has been shown that if ever a population stops eating a whole food type of diet, or if people move to a country that eats as we do at present, then within a generation they get more cancer and atheroma and their teeth rot. The way we eat is killing us. It is not only cancer and atheroma that our diet promotes, but arthritis, allergies, varicose veins, diverticulosis and probably multiple sclerosis. Our diet encourages obesity – a killer in its own right – which causes problems such as diabetes, heart failure, wearing out of joints, thromboses and salt retention.

Technological advances help us to escape the consequences of an earlier way of life, only to fall prey to the consequences of the new way of life. It seems that nature catches up on us after a couple of generations, yet we continue to put expediency before principle.

TYPES OF FOOD

There are six kinds of food:

| Carbohydrates (CHO) | These are made of sugars bound together in long chains. As single sugars, they are sweet; when in the chains they are starchy. |

Fats	Mainly made of fatty acids and glycerine. They can be oils or solid.
Protein	Made up of amino-acids which contain amino-groups (NH_2) derived from plants and bacteria that bind atmospheric nitrogen.
Fibres	These are insoluble compounds that are indigestible but often unite with other substances in the intestinal tract. They are very condensed CHO. There are soft fibres, mainly found in fruit and vegetables; and hard fibres, mainly occurring in grains.
Minerals	Single chemical elements and a few salts.
Vitamins	Organic compounds not made by the human body and needed in small amounts to facilitate energy exchanges.

Each of these is essential but dangerous if taken to excess. A very important principle in eating and living is: not too much of anything. The Greeks first formulated this idea, using the phrase, *nothing too much*. Remember that. Balance and moderation are essential.

Food builds and maintains our bodies and provides us with energy for living. All these processes require small amounts of vitamins, minerals, and certain fats and proteins (see Chapter 4).

The amount of energy stored in food is measured in calories; these are a measure of the heat produced by burning up a gram of a substance. CHO is the main sort of food burnt by the body;

one gram supplies 4 calories. A slice of bread produces about 50–60 calories, a gram of fat supplies 9 calories and a gram of protein 4 calories.

EMPTY CALORIES

A food that supplies just energy (calories) and that lacks the nutrients essential for its use by the body, is not paying for its keep. We should totally avoid such empty calories in our diet. They have to steal from other sources the vitamins, minerals and enzymes needed for their use by the body, and so they produce deficiencies. Fat, sugar, starch and white flour products are such items. Because it contains 30 per cent fat, lean meat from an animal reared in captivity for eating falls into this category of empty calories. It has some nutrients but not enough to allow the body to use the fat in it without borrowing from other processes.

No type of food should be taken in excess of the energy requirements of the body because the excess is turned into fat. Signs of excess calorie intake are rolls of fat on the body or lumpy outlines, compared with people of the same age and sex. If these are present, more calories are being consumed than are needed. It doesn't matter what you weigh; some people with big muscles and dense bones weigh much more than the average and yet are perfectly normal. The same applies to people with little muscle and light bones.

Suppose you are being careful about the empty-calorie intake and not eating too much protein and fat, and yet have excess fat on your body because your total calorie intake is too high. You may then feel unwell in various ways – a bit tired, irritable, nervous and so on. This is because the turnover of the excessive amount of fat increases the body's need for enzymes, vitamins, minerals, proteins and essential fats. You have slight deficiencies of these things and so feel unwell. This could be corrected by eating more fresh vegetables to compensate for the deficiencies. You might feel better but then get fatter and fatter and run into the problems of fluid retention, joint breakdown, shortage of breath, heart failure, thromboses and, because the pancreas can no longer make enough insulin to cope with the sugar turnover in a vast body, diabetes. However, not all diabetics are of this type; sometimes the pancreas fails for other reasons and of course so do the joints and heart.

On the other hand, if you eat moderately of the wrong sort of food (mainly empty calories in excess) you may remain thin but you will be nutrient deficient and feel unwell, or even develop obvious deficiency diseases. The poor answer to this situation is to carry on eating as you have been but to take vitamin and mineral pills to correct the deficiencies. But you have to take such a lot of the pills that it becomes a nuisance, and it is expensive, so most people don't keep this up. Even if you do continue pill-taking, the intake of additional nutrients is still short of what is needed. You are then a bit better off than you were, but are still not properly fed.

If you are overweight and eat mainly empty calories you are in a dangerous situation. Try to starve yourself and the deficiencies get worse, because safely burning up fat needs a lot of extra nutrients. You may feel so awful you cannot continue with the crash diet. If you have a strong will, you may make yourself ill. The safe way is to switch over to the Get Well Diet described in Chapter 6 and then gradually cut down your CHO intake if the stopping of empty CHO and fat and calories has not done the trick.

SUMMARY

A hundred and fifty years ago the people of Britain, Europe and the United States got their calories mainly from CHO. Each individual's sugar consumption was about 6 lb per year; the intake of wholemeal bread and flour amounted to about 370 lb in the same time. Not many vegetables were taken uncooked. If the calorie intake was high enough, this diet provided just enough nutrients, though iodine, zinc and selenium were short in areas where the soil lacked these elements. Vitamin D could be deficient when there was little exposure to the sun.

Today the consumption of sugar is up twenty times, fat up five times, protein up a little; fibre is down by half. Almost all food is processed, taking on chemical additives but losing its basic properties and many nutrients. We live on empty calories, de-natured food and many new, unnatural additives.*

Undertakers have noticed that dead bodies last three or four days longer than they did 50 or 60 years ago; this is because they are packed full of the preservatives which almost all bought cooked food and commercial frozen foods contain.

We have a higher cancer and atheroma death rate, but less vitamin D and iodine deficiency. Gross vitamin deficiencies, once prevalent, are now recognised and are therefore largely prevented. But not enough people know of the possibility of chromium, zinc and selenium deficiencies, and these are common. Mild multiple deficiencies of minerals and vitamins are frequent. It is being gradually realised that the vitamin requirements of individuals vary greatly. In some people these may be up to several thousand times the average requirement. If this fact was widely known, much mental ill-health would be preventable and curable. But people are held in the grip of their eating habits and dislike spending time on food preparation when they could be doing something else. So it is not just a simple problem of knowing what is best; it is a question of having to fight the habits of a lifetime to live in a state of health.

There is a little rhyme which ends, 'he was right, dead right, as he drove along, but he's just as dead as if he'd been wrong'. People like to think they are all right. 'How are you?' I bet you almost always say, 'I'm fine thanks.'

We're terrible liars too.

* Miriam Polunin gives a good summary of the additives in food in *The Right Way to Eat* (Dent, 1978).

3
FINDING GOOD FOOD AND KNOWING WHAT TO AVOID

Plants and vegetables take all their nutrients from the soil and so the goodness has to be put back into the soil. The ideal vegetable food is grown in soil kept fertile by compost and natural additives only. No artificial fertilisers or agricultural sprays should be used. The latter deposit toxic residues on the plants, which we ingest; as these sprays are meant to attack organic life, they will also poison us. Excesses of nitrogen and phosphate, especially the former, lock up some metals (magnesium is the chief of these) in the soil so that plants cannot obtain them.

If adequate compost (i.e. plant, leaf and animal manure which has been broken down by bacteria into a finely divided, rich soil or compost) is not applied to the soil, the latter's constitution is destroyed and it blows away. This has happened extensively in the United States and is happening in Lincolnshire today. Soil should have regular crop rotation as well as having compost heavily applied to it. Unless this is done its quality slowly deteriorates.

There is mounting concern about this amongst the public, and increasing numbers of growers are producing pure compost-grown food. Prices must be higher, of course, since more plants are lost to pests, growth is slower and the land less intensively used.

WHERE TO BUY GOOD FOOD

There are very few shops that specialise in selling such vegetables. The best-known is the Whole Food shop in Baker Street, London, but there are several directories of wholefood suppliers and the names of these are given below:

The Organic Food Finder Guide (1983, £2.95)
The Organic Growers Association
Aeron Park
Llangeitho
Dyfed
Gives 300–400 outlets.

The Organic Food Guide (ed. Alan Gear, 1983, £2.50)
The Henry Doubleday Research Association
Convent Lane
Bocking
Braintree
Essex CM7 6RW
Also available from the Soil Association, Walnut Tree Manor, Haughley, Stowmarket, Suffolk: £2.95 including postage and packing.

The Organic Food Service Directory of Growers and Producers in the British Isles
Ash
Cherston Ferrers
Brixham
South Devon
Supplied free if you send an A4 SAE to the value of 32p.

The realisation that most of our food comes from unhealthy soil and is contaminated by pesticides might alarm some people and cause them to fear that they are poisoning themselves. To a certain extent this is true, but it is not as immediate and serious as all that. Under 5 per cent of all cancers are attributed to this cause. Exposure to such low-grade mineral-deficient, pesticide-covered plants only affects human beings slowly over many years.

MAKING THE BEST OF WHAT IS AVAILABLE

If you cannot get compost-grown, pesticide-free plants be sensible and make the best of what you have. Tell your greengrocer that if he could supply such vegetables you would be willing to pay more for them. When the public demand for such food is sufficient, growers will be encouraged to supply it. They are not insensitive to falling sales.

To deal with food that is polluted with sprays, you should wash vegetables in a fairly strong solution of vinegar and water. The acid solution gets rid of some poisons. Always rinse the vegetables thoroughly before cooking them. It is better to peel hard-skinned fruits before use because some organic chemical sprays are compounded in the skins and are not removed by washing. But for soft fruits and green vegetables the trick with the acid vinegar solution is helpful. Don't use good-quality cooking, cider or wine vinegar. Use ordinary vinegar and buy the cheapest – it is more acid than the better quality stuff.

If these precautions fail to reassure you, try to analyse the reason for your excessive anxiety. It may be based on some deep-rooted emotional stress.

WHAT TO AVOID

Now we come to a list of forbidden things. Do not take anything:

canned	the quality, life, minerals and vitamins in these foods are reduced
smoked	contains carcinogens
pressure cooked	destroys vitamins, leaches out minerals

bottled	quality, life and vitamins are low
preserved with sugar, salt, nitrates etc.	these three are dangerous
irradiated	damages food (free radicals)
with artificial flavouring	organic chemicals may be poisonous or allergenic
with preservatives	organic chemicals may be poisonous or allergenic
with condiments, i.e. salted	excess salt is dangerous
treated with sulphur or sulphur dioxide	SO_2 is a poison
with colouring material	the organic chemicals used may be poisonous
with manufactured sauces	the organic chemicals used may be poisonous
commercially prepared and frozen	all contain preservatives

All these methods of treating food damage its quality. Vegetable food has life in it when it is fresh, but when it is heavily cooked and treated and stored it loses this life. Commercially prepared frozen food has been kept a long time, and almost all of it has added preservatives and antibiotics to improve its shelf life, so do not eat it. For the short term you can freeze your own produce, but the longer you keep it the more life it loses.

Herbs used for medical treatment and plants used for food have two kinds of quality: first, the quality that is associated with their life force; and second, their chemical constituents and vitamin and enzyme content. When a plant or an animal dies, the life force departs from it after a while – up to 48 hours or a bit longer – and it then deteriorates according to the laws of physical chemistry. It is next invaded by bacteria which eventually decompose it. When used as medicinal substances, herbs have two types of action: the 'life' one and the chemical one. They are therefore better than tablets for which the active principle has been chemically extracted and isolated. This isolation is the reason why drugs often have a toxic effect. When a drug exists in a plant, it is only one of many substances with a similar action and the plant often has other substances which balance the action of any one substance and therefore prevent the bad effects. The toxic effects of the drug are the result of breaking the principle of 'nothing too much'. These are the reasons why the types of food in the above list are forbidden.

Cooking Utensils

Cook in stainless steel, iron or enamelled ware only. Do not use aluminium or Teflon-coated utensils. You can take in an excess of aluminium and poisons are produced by heating Teflon. Some people are sensitive to aluminium. They get symptoms of irregular bowel action, odd gripings or just feel generally unwell. This can be cured by homoeopathic treatment.

Avoid Self-poisoning

Do not deep fry – it produces carcinogens in the oil. In fact fry as little as possible. It raises the fat intake too much (see pp. 89–90).

Give Up	Reason Why	Substitutes
Smoking.	Contains carcinogens, destroys vitamin C, damages the heart and lungs.	None.

Alcohol: when more than 2 glasses of wine, 2 half pints of beer or 2 tots of spirits per day are taken.	Alcohol is a depressant poison and like all such poisons it stimulates slightly in small doses. Up to the levels given, it has been shown to stimulate prostaglandin production.	Any fresh vegetable juice. Fruit juices on the Get Well Diet should be taken in moderation.
Coffee, tea, chocolate.	These contain stimulants and poisons which harm various organs and functions.	Herb teas and non-fluoridated water (Bottled spring waters are a practical solution).
Fluoridated water – check your supply with your local authority or Water Board.	Fluoride is a tissue poison and in excess produces cancer.	Change to a non-fluoridated water for drinking; current filters do not remove it entirely. Buy bottled water or install a still.
Avoid fluoridated toothpaste.	It can produce cancer in the mouth even in children.	Weleda do a toothpaste containing safe homoeopathic fluoride. Or use a non-fluoridated one.

Give Up	Reason Why	Substitutes
Applying chemicals to your body; e.g. hair sprays, make-up (some are safe and are advertised as such), deodorants, hair dyes and colour rinses.	Many of these contain poisonous chemicals. Some carcinogens and poisons are easily absorbed through the skin.	None, except for some safe make-up products.
Detergents for washing up.	Even those marked as biodegradable last 72 hours. Detergents remain on the surface of crockery and work by breaking up molecules. This produces very active pieces of larger molecules called 'free radicals'. These interfere with normal body functions, genes during cell division, and so on.	Soap flakes, or wood ash which contains potash and forms soaps with the fat on the utensils, or just brushing in hot water with 'elbow grease'.

4
THE CHEMISTRY OF FOOD

This chapter is for anyone who is interested in examining in detail the reasons why such radical changes to the average Western diet are suggested in this book. If you simply want to know what to eat to get well again or to prevent illness, then Chapter 2 provides all the basic information you need.

CARBOHYDRATE

The word carbohydrate is compounded from the words carbon, oxygen and hydrogen; I shall refer to it as CHO in future. There are three kinds of CHO – sugars, starches and fibre; all contain hydrogen and oxygen in the ratio of 2:1.

CHO was the first component of our diet to be studied. In terms of quantity consumed CHO is the most important portion. We consume roughly 10 units of CHO for every unit of protein. Most of the energy of the body is produced by the burning up of CHO internally, combining it with oxygen to produce water and carbon dioxide eventually, but it plays no part in the structure of our body unless as fat. Only if we eat CHO in excess of our energy requirements does the body turn it into fat and store it; otherwise it plays little part in the main body chemistry, such as the production of protein, hormones, enzymes and other metabolic processes taking place in growth and body maintenance.

Sugars

Sugars are of two kinds: monosaccharides and polysaccharides.

The monosaccharides are the basic units of sugar, being

simple short chains that cannot be shortened further in the body. They are known by the number of carbon atoms in the chain. Some of the chains loop together to form rings. There can be sugars containing nitrogen, called the amino-sugars. Some sugars lose oxygen and form alcohols.

The polysaccharides are built up through combinations of monosaccharides. They are used for storage and the formation of cellulose and lubricants in the human body. They also turn into *fibre*, which takes part in the structural components, and starches, the form in which CHO is stored in plants.

It is necessary to distinguish between refined and unrefined CHO – white flour and white sugar are the main sources of refined CHO but so are *starches* in the form of semolina, ordinary starch and potatoes without their skins. In its production white flour is almost entirely stripped of its nutrients, though some of them are put back. White sugar remains totally stripped of all its nutrients. These substances, therefore, are empty calories. They do not contain the nutrients to service their utilisation (see Chapter 2) and are dangerous. Try not to eat any of them; they rob the body of nutrients.

Unrefined CHO

These are the only form that should be eaten. They contain their own nutrients, vitamins and minerals plus their fibre. They are not dependent on other sources for these. Whole grain, including brown rice, wholemeal flour, peas and beans, lentils which have their skins, nuts, dried fruit, root vegetables, fruits, and leaves. Fruit and vegetable juices also contain them but they have lost some of their nutrients in the process of juicing. The less refined the CHO is, the more slowly it is used by the body. Thus it does not require the over production of insulin to correct high levels of blood sugar such as are found if large amounts of sugar, or even large amounts of fresh sweet fruit juices, are taken. This mechanism is discussed in Chapter 2.

Fibre

While the other types of CHO are easily digested and rapidly used, fibre is not digested and passes through the intestinal tract unchanged. There are a number of different types of fibre, graded in degrees of softness. There is hard fibre which is found in bran and soft fibre which is found in fruit. There is no point in just shovelling bran on to your food, because it tends to produce hard stools and upsets some people's bowels. What is needed is a balanced mixture of hard and soft fibre. This is best achieved by eating a mixed diet of whole grains, and fruit and vegetables that also contain ample supplies of fibre especially of the soft type intermediate between that found round seeds as fruit and the hard fibre in bran. Again, the principle 'nothing too much' applies. The right amounts of the right sorts of fibre, contained in a natural wholefood diet, tend to absorb the water in diarrhoea, as well as providing bulk in the stool and preventing constipation, so that the eater of such a diet enjoys the passage of a soft, formed stool.

If you eat the right amount of fibre you feel more satisfied by food, the bowel moves regularly, dangerous residues of animal protein do not linger in the colon and irritate it through fermentation. Therefore the incidence of carcinoma and diverticulosis is reduced. Also the growth of the correct micro-organisms of the bowel is encouraged so that nutrients can be made and absorbed there.

It has been argued in the past that eating a lot of fibre in wholegrain foods reduces the absorption of various essential minerals, such as iron and zinc, because the high fibre diet from whole grain contains phytic acid which combines with these elements. However, in subsequent research it was demonstrated that, once the body is accustomed to this diet, absorption of the minerals is perfectly adequate because the phytic acid breaks down lower down the intestine.

Incidentally, a secondary bonus is a reduction in varicose veins and piles because people do not strain. Piles plague impatient people. After the initial pressure that is needed to start a bowel action, lean forward and relax. Your bowel will do it for you. In fact, you can even train yourself not to make that initial push; just let your bowel do the work. Don't bother to buy any of the bran or cellulose preparations that are on the market – they are just commercial gimmicks. But do make sure that you have a wide range of fibre in your diet.

PROTEIN

Protein is the most important constituent of our bodies and in our food. Without it life on earth could not exist. Its name comes from a Greek word meaning first.

It has two main functions. The first is to make chemical exchanges inside the cells and manufacture other substances. For instance, the substances DNA and RNA are proteins from which the genetic pattern and behaviour of the cells flow. The second function is that of forming structures. Proteins are the largest molecules in the body. The inner structural framework of the body is built on strands of this substance. Bones grow upon a network of protein strands on which calcium phosphate is laid down, just as iron rods are the internal network around which concrete is poured into moulds to form the rigid outline of a building. Our hair and nails are made of protein. Our internal organs are filled out by protein, fat and CHO, but the network of fibrous tissue which makes the form is protein.

Proteins are made up of a combination of nitrogen, hydrogen, carbon and oxygen. The main characteristic is the nitrogen and hydrogen combination called an amine group (NH_2). This is derived from a combination of nitrogen from the atmosphere and hydrogen from water by 'nitrogen fixing' bacteria in the soil. These form ammonia (NH_3) which is absorbed by plant roots. Without this mechanism, the bacteria, plants and animals could not exist. In plants NH_2 groups are attached to long chains of carbon atoms to make amino-acids. From ammonia the word amine is derived and each amino-acid contains at least one atom of nitrogen, many carbon atoms with their associated hydrogen and oxygen atoms, and sometimes sulphur. The shapes of the proteins vary from the straight chains of carbon atoms to circles of carbon atoms like the sugars which contain six carbon atoms. There are also rings in which nitrogen, as well as carbon, is one of the single components. These frequently form a five-sided structure often found in enzymes, vitamins and steroid hormones. Protein molecules get so enormous that they cannot pass through cell walls and live permanently in cells. If you take a single molecule of water as an example and assume its molecular weight is one, a protein molecule can be more than 50,000 times as heavy.

All these very complex life-supporting structures are derived from 20 amino-acids and most of these can be converted one into another as the need arises in the body. However, there are 8 which the human body cannot make on its own in this way. These are called the essential amino-acids (EAA). Any amino-acids that are not needed in the construction of the body can be burned as fuel but this is not a clean-burning type of fuel like CHO. Using protein for energy production is just like using coal as a fuel – a lot of nasty smell and acid smoke are produced and clinker is left behind that is not easy to dispose of. Much of the nasty smell comes from the sulphur components. Just think of rotten eggs, the smell of which is due to one of the breakdown products of sulphur containing protein called hydrogen sulphide. Something similar to this happens in the body. Too much heat is produced giving the well-known specific dynamic action of protein. The end product of this metabolism is uric acid. Sometimes the kidneys are unable to excrete all the uric acid produced. This can be deposited round joints, and even clog up the kidneys, in people with an insufficient supply of enzymes to break down the uric acid, and the disease called gout is produced. Too much protein probably also causes a tendency to high blood pressure.

There are a number of fallacies stuck in the minds of people generally and often, I am sorry to say, of dieticians too. One is that vegetable protein is second class and the only good source of protein is meat. By weight, steak is only 17.4 per cent complete protein and it also contains 25.3 per cent fat so, as a food, it is unbalanced. Its excessive consumption leads to a dangerous consumption of fat which gets deposited in the body's stores and arteries, interferes with the metabolism of essential fatty acids, and steals vitamins and minerals from the rest of the body (see the section on Fats, pp. 35–9). In general all red meats are not the best sources of protein, though it may be necessary to eat a little of them if you are the type of person that cannot manufacture your own protein from vegetable sources, as has been discussed in Chapter 1.

The most efficient animal protein is found in eggs which produce a higher proportion of usable protein than steak.

Furthermore the egg is quite a good source of vitamin B12. One egg contains almost all the daily requirement needed to prevent the development of pernicious anaemia. At this low level of intake 90 per cent of vitamin B12 is absorbed because the higher the intake of vitamin B12 the less is absorbed. An egg is much more economical to produce than meat from four-legged animals which require far more food than hens. Soya bean contains more protein which is totally usable (i.e. it is complete protein with all the 8 essential amino-acids in it) than any meat. It has by weight 34 per cent protein, and 18 per cent fat of which 11 per cent is polyunsaturated. However, it is always necessary to have a mixture of different types of vegetable protein in one meal (see p. 90), when vegetable sources of protein other than soya are used.

There are other points about protein which are not fully realised by chemically based nutritionalists. If typical menus from around the world are based primarily on grains and vegetables, peas and beans (with only about a tenth of the protein coming from meat, milk and eggs), it has been found that a diet sufficient to supply 2,500 calories a day, which is an ample intake for most people, would supply one and a half times the protein needed by 98 per cent of the population. It is very difficult on a mixed vegetable diet to produce a loss of body protein unless high levels of sweet things and other protein-free foods are taken. So there can be absolutely no danger of being short of protein if you eat vegetables, provided you do so sensibly and follow the instructions given in Chapter 2. In percentages of the calories provided, a slice of lean ham is about 25 per cent protein and the remaining 75 per cent is fat. If you have a carefully trimmed, lean, cooked piece of beef it will contain 65 per cent protein and 35 per cent fat, but untrimmed it is 24 per cent protein and 76 per cent fat. Wholegrain bread contains 14 per cent protein, only 9 per cent fat and 70 per cent CHO, and cooked beans contain 36 per cent protein, less than 6 per cent fat and 58 per cent CHO. People who are vegetarians, such as many Seventh Day Adventists in America, suffer far less from cancer and heart disease than those who eat a great deal of meat. Also diverticulosis, a disease in which there are blow-outs in the lining of the large intestine through holes in its wall, is associated with eating large amounts of meat and taking only small amounts of fibre in the diet; so is cancer of the large intestine.*

There are several other points which arise from the study of Eastern attitudes to diet which are not considered in modern chemical dietary science. These observations are also supported by Rudolf Steiner and his followers, the anthroposophical movement. Plants turn minerals into substances suitable for plant life – CHO, fats and proteins. When people eat plants, the human body has to bring the organisation of these products up to the human level. Animals, when they eat plants, reorganise the plant to their particular pattern of animal life. Therefore, though to a chemist animal food might appear useful for getting essential amino-acids easily, it represents an additional task to the human being – the turning of animal protein into human protein.

This is more of a burden to human beings than eating plant protein which does not have the disturbing emotional features of animals. Any sensitive person who has experienced a wholly vegetarian diet and a heavy meat diet will recognise the differences made in themselves. Meat eating seems to make one more emotional, passionate, earthy, and one feels oppressed by it. I am speaking from personal experience, not from theoretical considerations. Two weeks of a heavy meat intake and I begin to feel heavy, slowed up and inclined to be irritable. I can eat a little meat without any problems, and at small levels it does give one a sense of vigour, but take more than a certain amount and the heaviness soon sets in. There is another thing too that is worthy of notice – the effect of too many beans. This not only makes you windy but beans in excess make me feel heavy and sleepy. Pythagoras forbade his followers to eat them.

As regards the total amount of protein per day, a human being can remain in good health on 40g when adult. When children are young, they need more protein because they are building their bodies. The average daily requirement is usually pitched far too high. In 1974 the US National Academy of

* *Diet and Nutrition: A Wholistic Approach*, by Rudolf Ballantyne MD, published by the Himalayan International Institute, Honesdale, Pennsylvania.

Scientists lowered the recommended daily protein intake for men from 70 to 45g and for women from 58 to 46g. All these figures still have large safety margins. In Britain the recommended protein intake stands at 65g for sedentary men and 93g for the very active; 55g for most women; and 75g for boys of 15 to 18, with 58g for girls of the same age. So don't fuss about protein. Be careful to get the right mix of things and you will still be eating more than you really need.

Sprouting seeds not only greatly increase their vitamin but also their amino-acid content. When sprouted, many seeds contain first-class protein and are equal to meat. The sprouts should be eaten raw. Heat destroys some amino-acids. Sprouted soya beans, starting off with a good quality protein, are an excellent source. Don't take too many of them. The vegetarian diet tends to be a little short of the amino-acid methionine, but brazil nuts are a good source. Other good quality protein sources are millet, buckwheat, barley and rice – all whole grain of course.

When on the Get Well Diet, you should eat no meat as a source of protein. It should be obtained entirely from vegetables. However, remember that this is not a life sentence, though you may like a vegetarian diet so much, because you feel so well on it, that you never go back to eating meat. At the end of the three months, you are allowed to move on to the Stay Well Diet. If you still feel that you need meat, you may have a little, but never as much as before. See the Get Well Diet and remember what was said in Chapter 1.

Bear in mind that a lot of pesticides are used for growing vegetables and animals don't eat washed vegetables. Also animals tend to concentrate residues of pesticides and store them in their livers and other organs, so much meat contains quite a fair amount of these substances. Therefore the more meat you eat, the more likely you are to get poisoned by pesticides. Animals who eat other animals and offal are even more prone to this problem. Meat, fish and poultry contain two and a half times more DDT and similar pesticides than do dairy products and 13 times as much as the average content of grains and vegetables.

FATS AND OILS

It used to be thought that fat was just the visible fat in the tissues, an inert substance; that it provided a store of energy which could be used up in periods of starvation; that it acted as supporting tissue to the organs of the body and the muscular framework; and that it helped to insulate the body from heat loss. It is far from inactive. Even the apparently inert stores are always being turned over. Small areas of brown coloured fat are sites of heat production due to intense chemical activity. They are mostly in the fat on the back of humans. Many of the steroid hormones and other chemical messengers of the body (hormones and prostaglandins) are made from fats. A large proportion of the nervous system is fat and there is an association between minerals and fatty metabolisms. In many diseases the visible fat infiltrates all the tissues.

Today fat is being studied very closely and new information is coming to light all the time. This interest has been stimulated because the current common killer of human beings is atheroma, the medical name given to what is commonly called hardening of the arteries. This is due to fat being deposited on and under the inner lining of the arteries often following damage to that lining or the formation of blood clots which stick to the lining. The death rate from this is roughly double that of cancer, the other major killer. Until just after the turn of the century, round about 1911, atheroma as a cause of heart disease was unknown. The current epidemic started then and is getting steadily worse. It is obvious that we have not yet found the reason for this but a lot of the evidence suggests that it is a disorder of fatty metabolism. There is a strong association between high fat intake and atheroma.

There are two kinds of fat in the body: the visible fat which I have just been talking about and the invisible fat. The former is largely only energy-producing and is solid and visible. The invisible fats have a totally different composition and function inside cells and also take part in constructing their membranes. The brain, spinal cord, liver, lungs, kidneys, pancreas, heart, spleen and all muscle, and in fact all other cells of the body contain these different sorts of fats. They are not made from protein, starch or sugar or from the visible fat of other animals, but have to come directly from plant sources. Hence they are known as essential fatty acids (EFA). Only very small amounts of EFA can be stored. The body's requirements of these substances are high. For instance, the brain consists of about 60 per cent fat of which 40–50 per cent is EFA.

All EFA originates in plants and, though the body can manipulate the fatty acids and build ones that are suitable for its own structure, it cannot make two or three basic types of EFA which must come from plants. The plant world produces the basic building bricks from which people and animals can build up their complex cell structures. The essential role of plants in doing so cannot be overemphasised.

So what is a fatty acid? A fatty acid is a chain of carbon atoms, sometimes branched, which ends up with an acid radical which is a carbon atom, two oxygen atoms and a hydrogen atom. It is usually written as C–C–C–C–COOH. In the visible fats of humans and animals the links, or bonds, are single and the fats are very stable. All the other linkages in the carbon atoms are taken up with hydrogen or other complicated groups and there is less possibility of making further linkages or breaking down as there is when there are double bonds between the carbon atoms. Such fatty acids are called saturated and are commonly known as SATFA. Some fatty acids have double bonds between a few of the common atoms in their chains. These are more active chemically and are oxidised more easily by taking up oxygen at the double link and becoming SATFA. Such fatty acids are called polyunsaturated fatty acids – PUFA, for short. When they go rancid (oxidise), PUFA produce carcinogens. Common sources of PUFA are fresh, pressed seed oils, but they also occur in the leaves of plants.

The important thing to realise is that all EFA are PUFA and come only from plants. But not all PUFA are EFA. The public, and even some scientists who ought to know better, seem to have got hold of the idea that all PUFA are important. This is far from the case. Only two PUFA are important – linoleic acid which is found in seeds, and linolenic acid which is found in leaves. Plant seeds contain 10–30 per cent oil, and 30–70 per cent of the fatty acid present may be linoleic. There is little linolenic acid in plant leaves. Growing points on plants usually contain both linoleic and linolenic acid in equal proportions. There is plenty of arachidonic acid in plant food and the body stores, but little linoleic and linolenic acid and no stores of these. In fact, it seems that in ideal conditions the only truly essential EFA is linoleic acid, for both arachidonic and linolenic acid can be produced by the body. However, in certain conditions this production fails, so these acids become essential.

These fats have important bearings on the type of food we should eat and emphasise the importance of eating lots of fresh growing points of vegetables and seeds. The seeds should not be old and are much improved by sprouting because this converts them into growing points and increases the content of these important EFA. That is why the diet described in this book contains a lot of such material.

Fats usually have the fatty acids connected to glycerol and there can be one, two or three fatty acids so attached. Some fatty acids are connected to molecules made of a combination of glycerol and derivatives of phosphoric acid which contain nitrogen. This particular group of fats, the phospholipids, is found mainly in the nervous system.

Waxes are of considerable nutritional importance and are not yet fully studied. They occur in the nervous system and are long chain structures occurring in waxy leaves, buds, twigs and the young growing part of the plant. They also occur in animal material and are present in the honeycomb.

Forty per cent of EFA is used for energy production in the liver; 60 per cent is used for the formation of cell membranes, especially in the brain, 60 per cent of which consists of such fats. EFA is also used for the formation of prostaglandins, which act on many processes as catalysts, or hormones (chemical messengers) all over the body. Their amounts are small but their actions are widespread and important. EFA have a vitamin-like action on the skin, circulation and the kidneys. These latter organs fail if there is an EFA deficiency because haemorrhages occur between the cells. Rashes appear, and the water permeability of the skin is increased causing it to flake off. There is also a high fat excretion from the skin. Other glands fail, notably the sex organs, the adrenal and thyroid glands. Chronic viral infections may, through increasing interferon production, stimulate the need for prostaglandin production and raise EFA requirements artificially. Virus infections can also damage cells so that they cannot make certain enzymes and this interferes with chemical processes.

Now here is another turn of this long and complicated story. There is a bottleneck in the fat-turnover of the body produced by the small supply of one enzyme which is all-important. This is delta-6 desaturase. The non-essential fats and the denatured vegetable oils compete for this enzyme with the EFA. A dangerous deficiency can occur because it is so easy to eat too much of the useless visible fats and not to eat enough of the EFA. The latter go off quite rapidly in the processes of cooking, and especially in all frozen, tinned and packaged foods, because the delicate double bonds between the carbon atoms in the PUFA are oxidised rapidly when exposed to air and heat.

The clear implication of this information is that to be healthy one should eat a lot of salads and raw vegetable sprouts which are actively growing, as well as seeds which are not exposed to oxygenation or have been long stored, or better still which are actively growing themselves as sprouts.

To sum up, keep the intake of animal fats and useless vegetable cooking oils and fats down to a minimum, and eat a lot of sprouting seeds and the leafy parts of plants.

Another twist to the story is that the only type of EFA which can be used are those which are bent at the double bond so that the fatty acid chains are on the same side of that double bond. Those in which fatty acids are straight, i.e. the acid chains, are on different sides of the double bond and are useless for transformation in animal bodies. Nearly all the margarines and oils prepared for commercial use are of no health value at all because the treatment which is given to such oils converts the bent form into the straight form and makes them useful only to the manufacturer. They are just as bad as animal fat. In fact, sometimes they are worse because, owing to the breakdown of the bonds, oxygen is taken up and carcinogenic epoxides are produced.

These facts are of importance, not so much in the production of cancer, because not much cancer is produced by such carcinogens, but in the prevention of coronary artery disease which kills twice as many people as cancer. In all recent major reports on the use of PUFA in the prevention of coronary artery disease there has been no significant difference between people who eat more PUFA and less SATFA. There seems to be just a slight difference in favour of the PUFA but this is compensated for by an increase in cancer, so the mortality rate remains equal. If people go on eating too much fat, and thus prevent the items essential for health being manufactured from the small amount of EFA they eat, the situation will not change. The answer is to stop eating so much fat. There are two lobbies – one for the dairy trade, to eat more butter; and the other for the margarine trade, to eat more 'marge'. Advertisements are cunningly worded to promote one or the other side. Pay no attention to either of them.

VITAMINS

The word vitamin comes from vital (meaning necessary for life) and amine (the NH_2 group). This name was arrived at because people thought at one time that all vitamins were amines, but this is not true. Nevertheless, it conveys the idea that some organic substances are essential for life.

Minerals are not organic, they do not have to be manufactured. They are more essential for life than vitamins because without minerals the organisms that manufacture vitamins could not exist. Minerals always have to come from our food but some vitamins, in suitable conditions, can be manufactured in the body, even though this may only be done by the bacteria which live inside the intestinal tract.

Vitamins and minerals need each other because they work together to facilitate all the chemical reactions that take place in the body. Some of them are used to form enzymes. Although vitamins in the main are not metallic compounds, one of them is. This is vitamin B12 which, at the centre of its molecule, has an atom of the metal cobalt. On the whole, vitamins and minerals work in little groups. For example, selenium facilitates the reactions that vitamin E takes part in; vitamin B6 and zinc also have an association; and the diet can be low in calcium provided there is plenty of vitamin D available. If vitamin D is in short supply, much more calcium is needed.

A favourite activity of governments is to try to determine the minimum daily requirement in order to be able to recommend the daily allowance of a vitamin which should be aimed at in the diet. But life is not that easy. Rudolf Steiner made this very clear in his writings; he said nature is always complex, never simple. The reductionist scientific approach, which thinks that the body is a machine that can be reduced to its components, each of which must have a function and therefore can be complete in itself, is never right. The more you split a thing up, the more you find complex inter-reactions between apparently widely divergent activities. There are no such things as fixed recommended allowances – even the minimums vary. If a life function is studied, some people will need more of a thing than other people. A few need a great deal, the average need a moderate amount, and a few people can get by on extraordinarily low amounts of anything that is being tested. When this is plotted in a curve, with the numbers at one side and the amounts along the bottom, the shape is always like that of a bell. Sometimes it is a fat bell, sometimes it is a very thin bell; but such is the natural, vitalistic curve obtained when anything alive is studied.

Excessive intake of one vitamin may put a strain on other vitamins, so that more are needed to cope. Excesses of one type of food will make great demands on other nutrients, both vitamin and mineral. The presence of disease or medical treatment or stress of any type, will raise the requirement level for some vitamins. For instance, Professor Dickerson of the Nutrition Unit of Sussex University has recently shown that treatment of patients with chemotherapy and X-rays raises their vitamin B and vitamin C requirements approximately threefold. This is probably why our patients at Bristol do very well when they are having chemotherapy; so much so that one or two cancer units have noticed this and recommend their patients come to us when they are interested in doing so.

Each individual has a pattern of his own and requirements of vitamins and minerals commonly vary as much as tenfold. In exceptional individuals the difference may be as much as two hundredfold. Once this has been realised, it is often worth while trying high vitamin dosage with people who seem to be in hopeless positions. This has led to a vast improvement in many people, often in psychiatric patients using niacin, but also in cancer patients with vitamin C.

It is far better, however, to get all the vitamins and minerals needed from food alone. Many doctors say it is perfectly all right to just eat a good healthy diet, but what is a good healthy diet today? Our eating habits, our agricultural and commercial methods do not provide such food. It also depends on how the food is cooked as to how many vitamins remain in it. In addition, some essential minerals may not be available to the food in the place where it is grown. Selenium, a mineral that prevents cancer, is an example (see p. 68). A wholefood diet will help. Being overweight, though, can cause such large vitamin and mineral demands that symptoms of deficiency develop. Recent estimates show that 39 per cent of all men and 32 per cent of all women – and between the ages of 60 and 65, 50 per cent of both sexes – are overweight. However, dietary supplements are a bore to take and can make you rattle around feeling like a pill-box, and still they don't supply everything that is needed. There are some people who are never going to bother about their diet. If they are going to be helped when they are mineral- or vitamin-deficient, the only way is supplementation. This can be very helpful.

The problem is a very difficult one and the only solution is through education. Everyone, consumers and producers, needs to learn to appreciate that something ought to be done to grow food in good quality soil containing as many of the required nutrients as possible, and not to put profit, or shelf life, or convenience before nutritional needs.

Vitamin A

Definition
Vitamin A is a CHO with a chain of carbon atoms with a carbon ring at the end. Carotene, which is its precursor in vegetable matter, has a similar structure but is a chain double the length with two carbon rings at either end. It is turned into vitamin A in the liver and stored there to be released as needed.

Functions
It is necessary for life, growth, the visual process and reproduction. It is necessary for the stability of the cell membrane and small particles within the cell. It is also needed for healthy

skin. It helps to prevent cancer and works with vitamins C and E to heal wounds.

Sources
Its dietary sources are leafy vegetables such as watercress, spinach, kale, broccoli, the outer leaves of cabbage and lettuce, and corn, apricots and peaches. It is also found in liver and liver oils, milk, butter and eggs. The oils from cod and halibut livers are particularly rich in it.

Requirement
The requirement of vitamin A is determined by body weight. The measurement is the international unit (IU) which consists of 0.3 micrograms (μg) of all trans vitamin A1. The international unit of beta- carotene is double this, at 0.6μg. This is presumably because beta- carotene is used for purposes other than just the formation of vitamin A, such as for neutralising mucoproteins produced by cancer cells. About 1,400 IU are needed by babies and this rises to about 4,000 IU for adults, and is a little higher during pregnancy and breast-feeding. Requirements of vitamin A are raised by cold weather, lack of thyroid hormone or diabetes. Food processing destroys about 40 per cent of it; and some chemicals such as nitrates attack it. Doses higher than about 50,000 IU a day can produce signs of poisoning.

Deficiency symptoms
Deficiency symptoms are night blindness, dryness and roughness of the skin, dryness of the mucous membranes, and the formation of defective bone and teeth during growth. In some African, South American and Asian countries the commonest cause of blindness is vitamin A deficiency leading to dry tissues which become infected. Vitamin A deficiency in pregnancy can cause congenital deformities.

Signs of excess (toxicity)
The signs of excess of vitamin A are loss of appetite, baldness, the shedding of the skin and mucous membranes, swelling of the bones, anaemia, enlargement of the liver and headache. Headache is the important first symptom of vitamin A excess.

The Vitamin B Group

The discoverer of vitamin B was in for a surprise – the number in this group is now moving past 17 possible candidates.

Vitamin B1 – Thiamine

Definition
Thiamine is a true vital amine. It contains two portions: a ring containing four carbon atoms and two nitrogen atoms; and a ring with three carbon, one sulphur and one nitrogen atoms plus a few other side chains. It is freely soluble in water but there are no reserves of it in the body and a constant intake is needed.

Functions
It acts as accessory to an enzyme – that is as a co-enzyme. It functions in the breakdown of CHO and other energy cycles and plays an important part in the production of stimuli in the peripheral nerves and in brain function. It is essential for the working of muscles, particularly in the heart, and is necessary for growth and healthy cells and for the production of blood.

Sources
Its dietary sources are whole grains, bran, brewers' yeast, many seeds (especially sprouting ones), nuts, eggs and liver. It tends to be destroyed entirely in cooking, especially when soda is added.

Requirement
It is affected by the energy output and by the calorie intake, particularly of CHO food when this consists of processed materials such as white flour. The requirement rises from about 0.5mg in babies to about 1.6mg per day in pregnant and lactating women. The average for adult men and women is 1.3mg. Ageing and alcohol, strenuous exercise, smoking, and a high intake of coffee, all increase the requirement of this vitamin.

Deficiency symptoms

Deficiency signs first start in the brain, with poor memory and loss of concentration, irritability, mental confusion and depression. Muscular weakness, signs of loss of sensation usually in the feet and legs due to loss of nerve function is preceded by discomfort there; then as the deficiency gets worse usually there is heart weakness with failure or sudden death. There is a rare type in which a marked loss of memory is the main feature without the other signs.

Signs of excess

When the dose is increased the excessive amount is rapidly excreted by the kidneys and no toxic overdose symptoms are reported. But it is not wise to take too much of any one vitamin. The B group in a general way seem to be interrelated.

Vitamin B2 – Riboflavin

Definition

Here is another vital amine. One carbon ring is attached to two other rings containing two nitrogen atoms. Attached to one nitrogen atom in the middle ring is a short CHO side chain. It is water-soluble and not stored in the body, being rapidly excreted if taken in excess. This will turn the urine bright yellow. Flavins tend to be yellow and sometimes fluorescent.

Functions

This vitamin takes part in the formation of a lot of enzymes. It is employed in the use of energy by the body. It is essential for growth, tissue maintenance and preservation of the function of the skin particularly at the junctions of mucous membrane with the outer skin. It is necessary for the formation of new blood.

Sources

Dietary sources are green leaf vegetables, tomatoes, potatoes, apricots, sprouting seeds, grains, brewers' yeast, wheatgerm and milk (but not the type which has been irradiated to produce vitamin D because this destroys riboflavin). Muscle meats also contain it.

Requirement
The requirement varies from about 0.5mg a day for babies up to 2mg in pregnant and lactating women, the average for adults being 1.6mg.

Deficiency symptoms
The first noticeable sign is the formation of tiny, wet, greyish wrinkles on either side of the mouth. There can also be some soreness of the subcutaneous junctions, and itching in the mouth, and round the front and back passages. The tongue can also be sore and purplish-red. Inflammation of the skin creases over joints and anaemia due to the depression of the bone marrow can occur. There can be some irritability and psychological symptoms.

Signs of excess
Symptoms of excess do not occur because, as the dose mounts, the surplus is rapidly excreted and the substance is not stored in the body.

Vitamin B3 – Niacin

Definition
This takes many forms but it is mainly a five carbon and one nitrogen atom ring with an amine group attached to one of the carbon atoms. This is one of the vitamins which can be manufactured by the body, which it does from the amino-acid tryptophane. The bacteria of the gut also transform tryptophane into nicotinic acid but it is doubtful whether the body makes use of this source. Enzymes that can perform this transformation from absorbed tryptophane occur in the liver and the blood cells, and this production is increased in pregnancy. Nicotinic acid is also called niacin. It is water-soluble and not stored in the body.

Functions
Niacin is responsible for hydrogen transport within the cell and forms the substance on which many co-enzymes work to do this. It is much used in the formation of energy and is involved with the whole metabolism of fats, proteins and

CHO. It is particularly important in brain function. Given in large amounts it causes flushes of the skin and has been used to improve the circulation in the elderly. Niacin also helps to lower the blood cholesterol but only in a high dosage.

Sources
These are much the same as any B group vitamin, being present particularly in growing plant tissue, sprouting seeds, brewers' yeast and some fruit. It is found in whole grains, some organ and muscle meats, fish, etc. It tends to be destroyed by heat, air and the action of water.

Requirement
The usual requirement varies from about 0.5mg in babies to 2mg in pregnant and lactating women, with the average for adults being about 1.6mg. All physical work uses it up and raises the requirement. Diarrhoea stops its absorption, as it does with many vitamins and minerals. Alcoholism will also increase its requirement, as will the contraceptive pill.

Deficiency symptoms
These frequently show themselves in mental disturbance, irritability and hyperactivity, and can go on to delirium, confusion and hallucinations. The skin also suffers in niacin-deficiency, particularly areas exposed to sunlight which become red and develop a rash. Later, brown-coloured pigmentation is common. The mucosal lining of the intestinal tract is also severely affected and chronic diarrhoea is a feature. Clinically it is known by the three Ds – dementia, delirium and diarrhoea. But none of these has to be present. Often hallucinations and suspiciousness are a feature and it is a cause of schizophrenic symptoms. Mouth ulcers and soreness of the mouth also occur when the deficiency is severe.

Signs of excess
The main one is severe flushing. Liver failure can occur, though more with nicotinamide than nicotinic acid. Most people will tolerate 1g, i.e. 1,000mg, three times a day without difficulty over long periods. However, if they are deficient in other respects, liver failure may occur readily. This usually manifests as jaundice and is reversible if the intake is stopped.

Vitamin B4

This vitamin seems to have gone out of fashion and it is difficult to find any information on it, but it does exist. It is a true vitamin – an aminopurine. It is a constituent of co-enzymes and nucleic acids and has been used to extend the storage life of whole human blood. Its common chemical name is adenine. However, it tends to be slightly toxic, producing a high blood uric acid and renal failure, although it does occasionally help some people with anaemia. So I wouldn't advise taking this one. Its main source is animal flesh.

Vitamin B5 – Pantothenic Acid

Definition
This is basically a chain of carbon atoms with an NH group in the middle and the acid COOH group at one end. It is a water-soluble acid which is destroyed by heat, acids and alkalis, but it is quite stable in foodstuffs during long periods of storage and little is destroyed during cooking.

Functions
It acts as a growth factor for a very wide range of living beings from bacteria to humans, which is one of the properties of a substance known as co-enzyme A. The latter takes part in an enormous number of reactions in the body connected with energy and the formation of fats, triglycerides and cholesterol as well as choline. It plays an important part in the formation of steroids in the suprarenal gland.

Pantothenic acid has been thought to be effective against the toxicity to nerves of streptomycin and is also reported to improve bowel function post-operatively. Some people also use it in large doses for treating rheumatoid arthritis. It is also said to influence the growth of hair but this is not certain.

Sources
It is formed by bacteria in the intestinal tract. An average normal diet provides ample supplies of this since it occurs widely in plants and animals, though animals themselves do not seem to manufacture it.

Requirement
No figures are known for the daily human requirement but, on the basis of animal experiments, it is probably 5–10mg a day.

Deficiency symptoms
Pantothenic acid is so widely distributed in foods that deficiency is practically unknown in humans. In an experiment, using a specially deficient diet and an antagonist, the subjects reported fatigue, headache, sleeplessness, nausea, pains in the limbs, muscle spasm and disturbance of co-ordination.

Signs of excess
These are not reported as pantothenic acid is rapidly excreted in the urine.

Vitamin B6 – Pyridoxine

Definition
This consists of a ring of five carbon atoms and a nitrogen atom. It is water-soluble, fairly stable, but is destroyed by heat and light. It also deteriorates when stored.

Functions
It is involved in over 40 enzyme reactions as a co-enzyme. It is important for brain and nerve function, the formation of blood, and muscle operation. It affects the growth of hair and is necessary for bodily growth.

Pre-menstrual tension frequently responds where there is an associated zinc deficiency. It may be helpful in sickness due to deep X-ray treatment. Morning sickness in pregnancy may also be helped. Pyridoxine supplements reduce the frequency of toxaemia of pregnancy. In animals, hardening of the arteries (atheroma) is produced by putting them on a pyridoxine-free diet. It may also help in treating schizophrenia.

Sources
It is found in grains and their products, brewers' yeast, egg yolks, pulses, seeds, organ and muscle meat. In fact it is very widely distributed. But it is almost entirely lost in the milling of white flour.

Requirement

This is proportional to weight. With both adult men and women it is about 2mg per day. It may go up as high as 10mg in pregnant and lactating women. Worldwide studies show that people with hardening of the arteries have low levels of pyridoxine. The Pill increases the need for it.

Deficiency symptoms

Irritability, depression, sleepiness and psychological disturbances are common. Sometimes affects growth in children. The peripheral nerves are rarely affected. Dermatitis, seborrhoea, and shedding of the skin of the mouth and eyes may spread all over the body, especially where there are skin folds and sweating. There can be inflammation of the mouth and tongue. The growth of hair may be disturbed. In some cases anaemia may occur but this is not common.

Signs of excess

It is rapidly excreted in the urine so these are rare. However, if a patient with Parkinson's disease is taking Levodopa (a drug commonly used in its treatment), high doses of pyridoxine can make the disease worse.

The Forgotten B Vitamins

About 25 B vitamins have been identified but many have been discarded, because either they were found not to be essential or they were identical with others already discovered. Therefore there is a gap between vitamins B6 and B12.

Vitamin B12 – Hydroxocobalamine

Definition

This is a unique vitamin for it is required in very small amounts and has a single atom of cobalt at its centre. It is very much a vital amine as there are no less than four nitrogen atoms surrounding the central cobalt atom. Another unusual feature is that though water-soluble it is not stored in the body.

Functions

The main function of B12 is to act as a co-enzyme in combination with folic acid to allow the maturing and release of red cells from the marrow into the circulating blood. It protects the myelin sheaths of nerves from damage. It is necessary for growth, the production of sperm and to maintain the integrity of mucous membranes, especially of the mouth.

Sources

It is manufactured by animals, bacteria and yeasts. Food that is of plant origin and is free from bacteria and yeasts contains no B12. Absorption of B12 in the human requires the aid of the 'intrinsic' factor, a muco-protein secreted by special cells in the stomach. Deficiencies can occur in people who eat absolutely no animal products (vegans), but some people can adapt to this situation by absorbing the vitamin from that which is produced by bacteria in the intestine.

Requirement

From 0.6–1.5μg is sufficient for adults. Children need double the latter figure, lactating and pregnant women need 5–8μg. The Pill and illness also increase the requirements.

Deficiency symptoms

The main disease is a severe large celled anaemia with a sore shiny tongue and tingling and numbness of the hands and feet. Degeneration of the spinal cord may produce weakness and lack of co-ordination of the legs and arms. Fatigue and shortage of breath are usually the first symptoms, but sometimes the spinal cord symptoms occur alone. Vitamin B12 deficiency may mimic schizophrenia.

The Folic Acid Group

Definition

Folic acid is the commonest of a number of similar compounds. It is a true and vital amine and is so named because it was first found in spinach foliage. It is classed in the B group of vitamins but for some reason has not been given a number. It is water-soluble and a little is stored in the body. It is very sensitive to heat and 50–95 per cent is destroyed in cooking.

Functions
Folic acid plays an important part in cell division, particularly in the formation of red blood cells, the genes (heredity factors) and the formation of some amino-acids.

Sources
Dark green leafy vegetables, whole grains, nuts, orange juice, turnips, brewers' yeast, potatoes, soya beans and meats.

Requirement
The requirements are small: for adults about 50µg, half this in a child and up to 500µg a day in pregnancy and lactation. Absorption may be blocked by the Pill. Old people do not absorb it well and may need supplements.

Deficiency symptoms
The chief one is a large celled anaemia like that of vitamin deficiency occurring mainly in pregnancy but also in old age. Mental symptoms, irritability, depression, insomnia, fatigue and poor memory are common, as is slow growth in children. There may be an increased susceptibility to infection.

Signs of excess
No such symptoms are reported. Because its use can mask the nervous damage of vitamin B12 deficiency folic acid should not be used indiscriminately or in large doses.

Para-aminobenzoic Acid – PABA

It is doubtful whether PABA is a vitamin. It is a part of the folic acid molecule. It sometimes can help people with vitiligo, a condition where harmless white patches appear on the skin. Scleroderma, a progressive thickening of the skin that is both uncomfortable and ultimately fatal may be helped by large doses. Care should be taken in its use for it can cause rashes, hepatitis and a shortage of white blood cells. Rich sources are molasses, brewers' yeast, wheatgerm, eggs and liver.

Inositol and Choline

These two little understood substances are considered to be part of the vitamin B group. They are connected with nerve function and fat deposition in the liver and arteries. Wheatgerm, brewers' yeast, brown rice, nuts, molasses, beefheart and brain, fish and soya beans are good sources.

Biotin (Vitamin H)

This substance is essential for life, but deficiency occurs only in unnatural circumstances such as a diet of raw eggs in adults. It is manufactured in the body by the intestinal bacteria and absorbed. Diarrhoea in infants can produce a deficiency and cause dermatitis, weakness, lack of appetite, nausea, muscular pain and localised numbness. Deficiency may also cause liver damage.

Bioflavonoids – Vitamin P, including Rutin

These are a group of substances widely distributed in plants, particularly in fruits rich also in vitamin C. They occur especially in the skins and pith of lemons, and blackcurrants. They strengthen the small blood vessels, and seem to increase the action of vitamin C. Apricots, grapes, green peppers and tomatoes are rich sources also.

The 'Not the Vitamin B' Group

Vitamin B10 – orotic acid.
Vitamin B15 – pangamic acid.
Vitamin B17 – amygdalin, incorrectly also known as laetrile.
All the above are not essential for life and are therefore *not* true vitamins.

Vitamin C – Ascorbic Acid

Definition
Ascorbic acid is not a vital amine, but consists only of carbon, oxygen and hydrogen, so it is a CHO. All animals make their

own vitamin C except humans, the great apes and three other odd little animals. It is not stored in the body and is water-soluble.

Functions

Ascorbic acid has a wide range of activities in the body; new ones are still being discovered. It is essential for the formation of collagen, the connective tissue that holds the cells together. It is necessary for the proper function of the immune system and the production of steroid hormones. It has an anti-viral and anti-bacterial effect. It stimulates mental function and gives more energy. It aids the excretion of metallic poisons. Ascorbic acid achieves all this by virtue of being a strong reducing agent, an acceptor of hydrogen ions and a donor of hydroxyl (OH) groups. Being so active chemically it is easily destroyed by heat (cooking), air and light.

Sources

Good sources are citrus fruits, rose hips, green peppers, broccoli, spinach, tomatoes, watercress, parsley, sprouting seeds and grains. Potatoes are a useful source in the winter.

Requirement

The minimum daily intake to prevent scurvy is about 10mg for infants and adults. Gradually opinion is swinging away from this rather conservative estimate and in recent years the re-commended daily intake has steadily risen; writers are now speaking of 60–100mg per day with up to 250mg for workers in very cold climates*. To achieve such levels supplementation is needed. Many people interested in good health now take 500 or 1,000mg per day.

Deficiency symptoms

Fatigue, lack of ability to respond to stress, a liability to infections, dryness of the skin with enlargement and scaling of the hair follicles most noticeable where clothes rub the skin, are the common early symptoms. Anaemia, and a tendency to bruises followed by the severe symptoms of scurvy, haemor-rhages from the gums and into the bones, loss of teeth and

* *Geigy Scientific Tables* Ed. K. Dien (Lentner 7th edn. 1970).

complete prostration. Long-term effects of milder deficiency are anaemia, fatigue, changes in the bones, poor teeth, atheroma (hardening of the arteries) and cataracts. Sudden death can occur with Vitamin C deficiency. There is some evidence from Australia that 'cot deaths' or the sudden infant death syndrome may be due to this cause.

Signs of excess

Vitamin C is well tolerated in large doses (10–12g a day); above this level it is rapidly excreted and oral dosage becomes increasingly more uneconomical. Non-buffered vitamin C in large amounts can produce diarrhoea and acidosis. These are reversible on stopping the intake, so they are not important.

Vitamin D

Definition

The vitamin D family are practically all composed of hydrocarbons, as they contain only one oxygen atom. Animals make them readily from cholesterol and similar compounds in the skin, provided the latter receives enough ultraviolet light. Strictly speaking, therefore, they are not essential for life unless there is insufficient exposure to sunlight in one's living conditions. They do not dissolve in water but are soluble in fat. Vitamin D2 is the most effective of the vitamin D group. All members can be stored in the body.

Functions

Inside the cells of the body, vitamin D causes the release of calcium in the chemical factory units called mitochondria. This makes it play a part in the functions of bones, heart, nerves, energy production and kidneys, as well as helping to maintain a normal blood level of calcium, together with the parathyroid glands and calcitonin.

One of its main functions is to encourage the absorption of calcium from the food. If there is sufficient vitamin D, enough calcium to maintain health can be obtained from a very low intake. The other main function is for the development of normal bone and teeth. It also favours the absorption of magnesium.

Sources
The natural source is sunshine. Food sources are fish liver oils, sunflower seeds, eggs, fish and milk. All plants contain a substance like vitamin D2 with a tenth of its activity.

Requirement
Unless a person does not go out of doors enough, lives in a country near the North or South Poles, is pregnant, breast feeding or growing, natural production of vitamin D is sufficient; otherwise 400 international units (IU) of vitamin D is required. One IU is 0.025μg of crystalline vitamin D3. The toxic effects of vitamin D overdose appear when the intake is more than 3,000 or 4,000 IU per day. This is easy to achieve when fish oils are taken freely and sometimes occurs with margarines and baby foods, to which vitamin D is added. The Pill tends to block its action.

Deficiency symptoms
Nervousness, cramps and spasms, pains in the long bones or back, followed by bending of the bones and thickening of the areas towards the ends of bones where growth takes place, the piling up of uncalcified tissue, with prominence of the forehead, are the picture of developing rickets. Sometimes the muscular spasms are of long duration and are called tetany. One common, easily recognised sign, is prominence of the growing point of the ribs which is where the bony ribs join the cartilages that join them to the breast bone. This can be felt or seen in children. It looks like a necklace of wooden beads and is called the 'ricketty rosary'.

Signs of excess
All the members of the vitamin D family are toxic in excessive amounts. They free the calcium from the bones and this raises the blood calcium and increases the excretion of phosphate and calcium in the urine. This calcium is taken up particularly by the blood vessels and kidneys, but is also deposited in any soft tissue.

Symptoms are loss of appetite, stomach and gut symptoms, headaches, joint pains, weakness and lassitude, muscular irritability and a raised blood pressure. Death is usually from kidney failure.

Vitamin E

Definition
This is another group of similar, oily compounds, called tocopherols, of varying degrees of activity. Basically they consist of two carbon rings, one with oxygen replacing one carbon atom. Joined to the latter is a hydrocarbon chain of 13 or more carbon atoms. They are not amines, are stable to acids, alkalis and heat, but take up oxygen readily. They dissolve in oil but not water. All members of the vitamin E group are stored in the body.

Functions
The actions of this vitamin are not yet fully understood and are wider than was thought originally. It is not just essential for fertility. It acts as a preservative of unsaturated fatty acids (PUFA), vitamins and enzymes because it takes up oxygen so easily. It also, by virtue of this feature, acts as a co-enzyme and takes part in energy exchanges. It helps the heart to use oxygen and prevents thromboses, and is developing a reputation as a preventative of ageing and the effects of radiation.

Sources
Especially found in growing plant tissues, sprouts and unrefined seed oils, especially wheatgerm. Almonds, walnuts, parsley, broccoli, asparagus, spinach and eggs are also good sources.

Requirement
An adult requires 10–30mg of alpha-tocopherol per day. This is sufficient for pregnancy and breast feeding. One old international unit was 0.73–1.10mg, depending upon which tocopherol was available. Some people seem to do better on more – up to 1,200mg per day has been recommended. But care is needed – high doses sometimes raise the blood pressure too much. Start with 100mg per day and increase slowly under

medical supervision in cases of high blood pressure, diabetes and heart disease.

The Pill and mineral iron (as opposed to natural iron in plant and animal food) antagonise vitamin E. Extra vitamin E is needed in people taking these two substances. People taking refined vegetable oils need more than average amounts of vitamin E, so should those with defects of fat absorption.

Deficiency symptoms
These are not particularly marked in humans but can be severe in experimental animals, varying with different species. Pigmentation, anaemia and clotting of blood vessels may be signs of mild deficiency.

Signs of excess
Apart from the possible side effects mentioned above, the tocopherols do not appear to be toxic in large doses.

Vitamin F

The essential fatty acids (EFA) have been called vitamin F. They are dealt with fully in the section on Fats and Oils earlier in this chapter (see pp. 35-9).

Vitamin K Group

Definition
These are very similar in structure to vitamin E but are quinones. They are fat-soluble, fairly stable to heat but unstable to light. They are stored in the liver and spleen.

Functions
They are necessary for blood clotting by affecting the formation of prothrombin and other blood clotting factors.

Sources
Both from the green leaves of plants and from the bacteria in the intestine. Bile is needed for the absorption of these vitamins, so deficiency can occur in obstructive jaundice, also in

diarrhoea and antibiotic therapy that damages the intestinal bacteria.

Requirement
Ample amounts are available, except in the newborn. Supplementation is only given routinely in premature babies, and except for conditions which produce a prolonged clotting time due to vitamin K deficiency, it is not otherwise required. It is not desirable to increase the tendency of the blood to clot.

Signs of deficiency
Bleeding that does not stop.

Signs of excess
Excessive clotting of the blood.

Vitamin P

See Bioflavonoids on p. 52.

MINERALS

Rudolf Steiner once said, 'Nature is never simple, always complex.' The vitamins were once thought of as amines that were essential for life. In the preceding section, it has become clear that this simple idea just is not true. Most vitamins are not amines and many vitamins are not single compounds but groups of similar compounds. In this section it will be seen that minerals are not just mere compounds which form the structure of the body; they are often very active components of energy exchanges, of vitamins and, just as many vitamins are, of enzymes also.

The more one looks into the details of nutrition, the more complex and difficult to understand it becomes. Steiner was absolutely right. One needs to grasp certain principles such as those scattered through this book – 'Nothing too much', 'Heating destroys vitamins', 'Too much heating produces carcinogens', 'Wholefood contains its own nutrients', 'Refining food produces empty calories' and 'Don't sacrifice principles for expediency', which means no ready-prepared or junk food.

Adding to the elaboration of the role of minerals in nutrition is the fact that amino-acids and vitamins have become available in pure form. This has made it possible to demonstrate the existence of many elements and compounds, only traces of which are essential for animals; because animals do not thrive on an apparently adequate mixture of pure vitamins, amino-acids, fats and CHO. Methods of analysis – for example spectrophotometry – have improved the isolation of individual minerals from complex mixtures. Hair and whole blood analyses have allowed more meaningful studies of the exchanges going on in the body than simple estimations of the concentrations of elements in the fluid compartment of the body alone.

Hair analysis gives information about the actions of minerals within the body three to six months before the sample was taken. Whole blood analysis gives information about the present transport of minerals and their deficiencies because it reveals the overall levels in both the cells and fluid compartments. By correlating these three types of information many new relationships have been found between minerals and this has led to the earlier detection of many deficiencies and excesses in mineral intakes.

Calcium

There is more calcium in the body than any other mineral, although phosphorus runs it a close second. Both are stored in teeth and bones as calcium phosphate. It is needed for nerve conduction, growth, formation of bones and teeth, prevention of blood clotting and the control of fluid passing through cell walls.

Its absorption is dependent upon adequate vitamin D. It is excreted during bed rest and after the menopause, when there is lack of oestrogen, for both of these situations lead to its release from the bones. This causes raised blood levels of calcium which can then be deposited in other tissues. Too much calcium can lead to clogging of the blood vessels and kidneys. Growth, pregnancy, exercise and lactation increase the body's demands for calcium. The average adult needs about 5–600mg per day. At puberty, in pregnancy and lactation double is required. But people can remain healthy on surprisingly less if the vitamin D intake is adequate.

Skimmed milk, whole wheat and its products, sesame and sunflower seeds, almonds, soya beans, sprouting seeds and grains and hard water are good sources of calcium.

Magnesium

Magnesium takes part in most chemical reactions in the body as it is incorporated in so many enzymes. It helps in energy production and transfer, in the formation of proteins and fats and in the use of calcium, potassium and sodium.

Acid soils tend to be deficient in magnesium and the now normal, heavy use of nitrogen to stimulate quick and plentiful growth of plants, locks the magnesium up in the soil so that the deficiency of the latter is common. The refining of food, use of water softeners, boiling of vegetables that dissolves it in the water and the use of preservatives in the preparation of frozen foods, further reduce the magnesium levels of the plants that are the source of this mineral. Only people who eat a lot of raw vegetable food get enough magnesium nowadays. Mild signs of deficiency are fatigue, irritability, poor memory and depression.

Calcium helps muscles to contract while magnesium helps them to relax. It is the natural calcium antagonist and, when delivered inside cells and combined with a transporter of mineral ions such as orotic acid, which does not release its magnesium ion until it reaches the mitochondria, can lower the blood pressure, reduce angina and the irritability of heart muscle and hence the tendency to bouts of irregular beating.

Alcohol, high protein, high fat and high refined CHO (e.g. sugar and flour) intakes, diabetes, kidney deficiencies, stress, pregnancy, lactation and growth all increase magnesium requirements.

It is hard to achieve an excessive intake of magnesium, as magnesium salts tend to be laxative, but this can be toxic. Requirements vary from about 65mg in babies to 450mg per day in pregnant and lactating women; 300–350mg is average for adults.

Iron

The formation of the oxygen-carrying protein haemoglobin cannot take place without iron, which is also needed for the formation of muscle haemoglobin. Many enzymes also contain iron.

At least one-fifth of the world's population is iron deficient and this burden falls mainly on women who lose blood regularly as well as bear and feed children. Children are born with small reserves of iron and easily become deficient as they grow.

Vitamins C and B, protein and copper in small amounts are needed for iron absorption. Foods 'enriched' with iron contain a type of iron that is hardly absorbed. The more easily absorbed iron can shorten shelf life because it discolours the product. The food preservative EDTA halves iron absorption. Phosphates used as additives in baked products, ice cream, soft drinks, sweets and beer also reduce iron absorption. People suffering from continuing blood loss, such as is caused by taking aspirin (losing about 5 tsp (5ml) per tablet), piles, nose bleeds and infections, easily become iron deficient.

Iron is the only essential nutrient, apart from vitamins A and D, whose richest source is in animals. Red meat, fish, wholegrain cereals and their products, dried fruits, green leafed vegetables, nuts, mushrooms and sprouting seeds are the best.

The symptoms of iron deficiency are mostly those of anaemia – tiredness and shortage of breath – but paleness, sore tongue and some nerve symptoms such as irritability, depression and tingling also occur.

Phosphorus

After calcium, phosphorus is the next most abundant mineral in the body. It is stored in the bones and teeth but is very active in the energy exchange systems of all cells and helps with the transport of fat. An average diet has ample phosphorus. It is better to avoid excess intake since when it is excreted it has to be joined to calcium which it takes with it and this can produce a deficiency of the latter. Therefore, avoid the sources of phosphates mentioned in the section on Iron.

Sulphur

Though some soils are deficient in sulphur, no diseases caused by sulphur deficiency are known. It is contained in four amino-acids and the only essential one of these is methionine. This is in adequate supply in both the Get Well and Stay Well Diets. Brazil nuts are a specially good source of methionine, but tend to produce allergy in some people and when sold de-shelled can easily become rancid.

Potassium, Sodium and Chloride

These three minerals are closely related. Sodium and potassium compete against each other and sodium and chloride are joined together to form common salt. Potassium is mainly in the cells and sodium in the tissue fluids. Excessive intake of sodium leads to a deficiency of potassium. Though the body requires only 500–1,000mg of salt a day, we eat far too much – about 10–12g a day. This is because salt adds flavour to food and we get the habit of taking more and more. Cooking and refining food takes out the potassium and the salt but only the salt is put back. So it is easy to develop a potassium deficiency which can produce fatigue, constipation and muscle weakness, especially of the heart. But sodium in excess causes swelling of the cells that leads to reduced kidney function and more swelling, so the blood pressure goes up and, with the associated potassium deficiency, the heart fails more. The answer is to reduce salt intake drastically and keep up a high potassium diet as described in this book.

Points to watch are: some sea salt is polluted; exposure to sunlight evaporates iodine from rock and sea salt; iodised salt, if freely added to food, may result in an excess of iodine; refined salt usually has an anti-caking agent added – acceptable if it is magnesium carbonate, but check this; Ruthmol is made only of potassium chloride – add this only after cooking, though some people do not like the flavour even then; Biosalt is a balanced mixture of salts, including iodine, and is best added after cooking; pills of straight potassium chloride cause duodenal ulceration; water softeners produce water with too much salt.

Iodine

The thyroid glands need iodine to produce their secretion, thyroxine. Thyroxine controls the rate at which cells function and hence optimum production, growth and mental function. A deficiency of iodine results in a reduced amount of thyroxine and an enlargement of the thyroid gland. The daily requirement is small – about 4mg (a teaspoon of kelp powder). Excess can cause rashes. Thyroid deficiency produces slowing-up mentally and physically, constipation, dry skin and hair, slow-growing brittle nails and in many people, obesity and oedema.

Iodine is found in all seafoods, animal and vegetable, dulse or laverbread (tasty with poached eggs), kelp, kombu, wakame, Hiziki (nice with rice and in soups), unrefined oils, Biosalt and spinach.

Zinc

Like iodine and selenium, zinc is short in glaciated soils, having been washed out when the glaciers melted. Pouring chemical fertilisers on the land locks up the zinc in the soil by forming insoluble compounds with it so that it is unavailable to the plants grown there. It is also removed by refining foods and by boiling vegetables when the residual water is thrown away. Excessive intake of fluid, particularly alcohol, leads to its excretion and coffee hinders its absorption.

Zinc is a constituent of many enzymes and takes part in many functions. It is essential for growth of bones and sexual functioning. It is also needed for good vision, appetite and sense of smell, the strength of collagen and fibrous tissue. Deficiency of zinc may mimic anorexia nervosa and possibly produce prostate enlargement and cause delayed wound healing.

The populations of countries that have been glaciated, especially those that suffer from modern agricultural methods, are all liable to mild or not so mild deficiencies of zinc. It is easy to spot and whole blood analysis will detect cases earlier than ordinary serum levels or hair analysis. Zinc should be, with chromium, selenium and magnesium, routinely estimated in renal dialysis patients.

The common signs of zinc deficiency are badly growing nails with horizontal white lines, often one month apart in women. In severer cases the nails are horizontally ridged. There are often white (old) or reddish (new) stretch marks on the skin particularly of breasts and buttocks. Menstruation may be infrequent and lack of sex drive and impotence frequent. Intellectual performance may deteriorate, with consequent psychological stress. The slow healing of wounds and ulcers, loss of the sense of taste and a lowered resistance to infection can also occur. Zinc deficiency is worth considering if there is no mechanical cause for infertility.

Some of the biochemical defects of schizophrenics produce an excessive excretion of zinc and vitamin B6. The administration of both these may relieve the symptoms of this distressing disorder.

The daily requirement of an adult is about 15mg of a zinc salt. Adolescents need the same amount; babies about 3mg and pregnant and lactating women need double the adult dose. The only currently available medicinal zinc product contains 200mg of zinc chloride; this frequently produces nausea and vomiting and nearly always diarrhoea. I have a preference for zinc orotate which is well tolerated.

The natural sources of zinc are pre-eminently oysters, followed by meat from mammals (best from various organs of the body), fish, shellfish, crustacea, beans and peas, seeds (especially sprouts of sunflower and sesame), nuts and eggs.

TRACE MINERALS

We now come to a group of essential minerals required in small amounts only, of about 1mg a day or less. Some have been known to be essential for over 50 years, such as copper which was first shown to be necessary in 1928. Today, with the tools available to recognise and measure very small quantities of single elements in a rich mixture of many minerals, the functions and relationships of these trace minerals, or elements as they are also called, are yielding startling new information about many hitherto baffling diseases. Cancer, atheroma (hardening of the arteries or arteriosclerosis), heart failure and diabetes are some of these.

Many people brought up on the chemistry of two or three generations ago, may find it puzzling that tiny traces of chemical compound may have such a profound effect and wonder why it is only the metallic part of the compound that is considered important. The acid part of a salt which is a compound molecule made of a metal combined to an acid, splits up in the body. Only a few acids are compatible to the body which tends to reject those that do not suit it – like Epsom salts or sodium sulphate. These acids should be considered as mineral, metal or ion bearers or carriers.

In solution many salts split up into ions. The metal has a positive electrical charge and the acid a negative charge. Some salts have the special property of not ionising until they reach a cell and can give up their positive metallic ion on the surface or inside the cell. This means that such compounds do not interfere with the constitution of the blood and tissue fluids altering its electrical charges, and interfering with other substances in those fluids until they get into the cells. Such compounds are often called 'mineral' or 'ion transporters'. The chemical combination of orotic acid with many metals provides a good example of a 'mineral transporter'.

It is the unique electronic composition of these trace minerals that makes them important. The vehicle they travel on to get into the body is like any other form of transport, an expendable unit that can be used for the movement of all sorts of more valuable loads.

Chromium

Chromium that is trivalent (i.e. has three points at which electrical exchanges occur) is necessary for the normal usage of sugar. If it is not available, diabetes occurs. It is also now being regarded as necessary for the prevention of atheroma (hardening of the arteries or arteriosclerosis). It is lost in food processing. It is present in whole grains and vegetables. Excess of refined CHO increases the body's need for it.

Cobalt

This mineral is the essential core of vitamin B12 (see pp. 49–50), otherwise there are no known conditions produced by its deficiency. However, in recent studies in the USA, violent criminals have been found to have low levels of cobalt.

Copper

It plays an essential part in many enzymes. It takes part in bone and blood formation, brain, nerves, connective tissue and functioning of the immune system. Zinc and copper are related. If there is too much zinc in the diet not enough copper is taken in and vice versa. Overloading with copper is easy, especially now that copper piping has replaced lead (a change to stainless steel would be an advance) and much acid water is produced by atmospheric pollution. The hyperactivity of some children and mental instability in adults is due to mild copper intoxication. Heart disease and hardening of the arteries occur frequently in animals with copper deficiency. Anaemia can be caused by copper deficiency. Green vegetables and sea foods are good sources.

Fluorine

This element is necessary for good teeth and bone formation, but there is a very narrow range between enough and too much. It does produce harder tooth enamel but only delays the production of tooth decay which is produced by eating too much refined CHO and not cleaning teeth properly twice daily. Furthermore, if there is more than just a little in the water supply, vegetables concentrate it causing bone damage and cancer. Fluoride intoxication also produces brain damage and other serious defects of all systems of the body.*

* *Fluoridation, the great dilemma* George L. Waldbott MD (Coronado Press Inc., Lawrence, Kansas, USA, 1978).

We get enough fluorine without adding it to our drinking water. It is a dangerous poison best left to natural supplies without interference.

Germanium

In Japan, a chemist who had discovered a method of preparing a soluble form of germanium had it tested and found it to be non-toxic. He discovered that it helped people with cancer and other serious illnesses that had been given up as terminal, and he started to use it at a small charitable clinic. Germanium seems to give a powerful restorative and healing boost to many body processes and then be excreted. It is starting to be used in Europe. Perhaps more will eventually be found out about this element.

Manganese

Manganese takes part in the functioning of many enzymes. It plays a part in bone formation, reproduction, nerve function, blood clotting and the metabolism of sugars and fats. Lack of it may produce arterial disease, diabetes and muscle weakness. The daily human requirement is 2–3mg. It is removed from foods by processing of all types. It is found in unrefined grains, vegetables, pulses, nuts and oils.

In industries where manganese dust is inhaled it can be toxic. The symptoms are irritation and infections of the respiratory tract, sleep disturbances, irritability, dermatitis, liver enlargement, widespread deterioration of the central nervous system with weakness, stiffness and tremor. An anaemia depression of the marrow can also occur and can be fatal.

Molybdenum

The bacteria that fix the nitrogen in the atmosphere require molybdenum to do this. No production of protein can take place without this process, so land that has no molybdenum will not support plant life. Molybdenum is essential for the life of mammals. Its main source is in wholegrain cereals and molasses and it is lost when these are processed. It prevents dental caries, which is why people who eat raw sugar cane have good teeth, may play a part in the formation of cancer of the oesophagus and in sexual impotence in older people. Excess of molybdenum may cause copper deficiency in sheep. Molybdenum can be used to correct copper excess but this reaction involves sulphur also.

Nickel

Nickel is essential for some animals but it is difficult for humans to have a nickel deficient diet. Nickel in contact with the skin as a component of cheap jewellery etc., often causes dermatitis. In industry combined with carbon monoxide, it can be very toxic, producing headache, vomiting, chest pain, cough and death. Chronic exposure can produce lung cancer. It is present in tobacco smoke – so is carbon monoxide.

Selenium

There is a lot of interest being taken in selenium at present, because a deficiency of it is related to cancer and heart disease. It is an anti-oxidant, that is, it prevents oxygen from combining with other compounds and damaging cells. It works with vitamin E in doing this. It helps the immune system to function and this may well be the way it prevents cancer. Papers are just beginning to appear that show that it can reduce the size of existing cancers in animals. Its activity in reducing the incidence of heart failure in selenium deficient areas, like Finland, has been studied.

Selenium deficiency is important because it is common in glaciated and soil eroded areas. It is destroyed by food processing. Where it is deficient in the soil, the whole cereals and organ meats (especially hearts), nuts, brewers' yeast, vegetables, unrefined oils and milk that are its normal sources, do not contain sufficient to maintain health. This makes selenium into one of the minerals it could be wise to take as a supplement.

It has been found that good health and a low incidence of cancer occur on a daily intake of 500µg per day. This suggests that about 200–400µg a day as a supplement would be about right for this country. Toxic symptoms do not occur until the intake is over 2,000μg per day.

The safest and most effective form of selenium to take is that obtained from a strain of yeast that binds selenium and incorporates it into its own cells. Brewers' yeast that has been treated with selenium compounds, and selenium compounds themselves or organic or inorganic compounds by themselves, are not so effective or safe. So read labels carefully and enquire if they are not clear. The term 'chelated' is often used. It means bound or joined chemically to another compound. It does not necessarily mean that it has been incorporated naturally.

Aluminium, Tin, Silicon, Vanadium and Gallium

With the exception of aluminium, all these have been shown to be necessary for growth of experimental animals but the application of this information to humans has not been followed up sufficiently to report on yet. Silicon, aluminium and tin in excess can be dangerous.

5
STARTING
THE DIET

It is my belief that psychological factors play a significant part in the onset of disease. For this reason I want to give encouragement as you set out to change the dietary habits of a lifetime. This is a tremendous task and nobody does it without the occasional lapse. Never feel guilty or upset about this; have a few indulgences and then go back to the job of getting well again.

To live, one has to manifest the attributes of life, and these are always to be active, positive and adaptable. Never give up! That is the secret. Having summed it all up in a nutshell, let's go into it in more detail.

It has always surprised me how people vary in their approach to changing their diet. Some people are very adaptable and make nothing of it, others have to work very hard on making the necessary changes. People often say, 'My instincts must be right'. But it's not your instincts that are talking when you say this, it's your habits. It is what you are accustomed to eating that has become the habit and formed your tastes.

For years you have been exposed to advertising and a subtle manipulation of your taste habits: your instincts haven't had a chance to develop.

*Technological Man, amongst other achievements, has devised a means by which our palates certainly, and our appetite possibly, can be deceived at the will of the provider of provisions; all he does is to insert the appropriate additives into what is eaten. In this way the learning of our palates can be circumvented. It happens every day.**

* Kenneth Barlow FRCR, DMR, MRCS, LRCP. *The Law and the Loaf* (Precision Press, 15 High Street, Marlow, Bucks., 1978), p. 53.

There are also other characteristics – your laziness, your inertia, your arrogance, your desire for self-indulgence, the fact that you may be ill and so not have enough energy to struggle with these habits – that make the difficulties when you want to change what you eat.

You will learn a lot about yourself which is of great importance if you take on the task of changing over to the Get Well Diet as part of resolving your disease or problem, whatever it is. Forty-five years of observing people have shown me that the way people tackle changing their diet is an important indication as to whether or not they will overcome their illness.

DIETETICALLY HOPEFUL OR MEDICALLY TERMINAL?

In the years before the Bristol Cancer Help Centre started I had met thousands of people with cancer. Of those who have apparently recovered, all but about 12 had had surgery, radiation or chemotherapy. All of those 12 people had had similar treatment to that available at the Cancer Help Centre. I have never seen a spontaneous cure of a proven case of cancer. They are rare. Today I am seeing a gradual change in the attitudes of cancer sufferers. More people are turning from allopathic treatment to non-toxic, vitalistic therapies. During the last two and a half years at the Bristol Cancer Help Centre I have been seeing more and more people who were told they were terminal by allopathic medical standards getting well again, mostly without any medical treatment.

What are the factors found in the dietetically hopeful?

1. *A strong desire to go on living because they value life itself*
Those who only wish to live for the sake of others are not in this class. They live from a sense of duty or love for others, but they are depressed and have basically given up.
2. *Spiritual awareness*
Most people who are spiritually aware value life for what it can teach them. They accept responsibility for themselves and can learn from the circumstances of their illness why they have become ill and the lessons it can teach them. This enables them

to transform themselves psychologically by changing to a new diet.

3. *Those who truly want to get well*

Those who have undergone great suffering, through illness or allopathic treatment, and want to get free of it will often willingly accept the diet. They have become able to overcome the mental defences they had set up against seeing themselves as they really are.

4. *Those of strong will*

Those who have inherited a strong constitution; who remain cheerful, humorous and calm under stress; who have normal personalities on the Lüscher Test*; and those who have had similar parents and a calm childhood are the people who can readily understand the need for a curative diet and carry it out.

5. *Loving support of family and friends*

People who are lucky enough to have such support, combined with a willingness to share the diet with the person who is ill, feel greatly sustained and make the change to the Bristol Diet easily.

What factors are found in the dietetically terminal?

1. *Lesions of the intestinal tract that prevent eating*

Cancers of the intestinal tract that have grown too large, the effects of previous operations, or large amounts of cancer or fluid outside the intestines but in the abdominal cavity can prevent the sufferer eating the Bristol Diet. The attempt has been made too late in the illness.

2. *Lack of understanding*

Some people never carry out any instruction exactly – they seem to have a built-in tendency to error. When this involves a fundamental part of the diet, this can lead to its failure. For instance, if a little of something is good, some folk will immediately assume that a lot is better.

To give one example: the need to clean, cook and prepare food correctly in the new way is important. Failure to do this will soon lead to a loss of appetite.

* *The Lüscher Personality Test*, by Ian Scott (Pan, paperback). This test, based on primary and secondary colour preferences, is used on every patient at the Bristol Cancer Help Centre.

3. *Lack of will*

People who cannot stick anything for more than a short time, or who really do not want to live, find it very difficult to continue on the diet long enough to change their habits. The person who has been introduced to the diet by a desperate relative is likely to have difficulty in developing sufficient will-power to finish the job.

4. *Lack of support from family and friends*

People whose families are disunited or selfish might receive no support and may often suffer direct opposition and ridicule. There is no loving care and understanding to sustain them. Such people have a difficult time. Though some overcome these difficulties when they are the cook, many do not, especially when they have to do it for themselves, isolated in their family home. This last situation is rare but very depressing.

A dietetically hopeful person

Bea Vernon was a member of the team that started the Bristol Cancer Help Centre. Her infectious enthusiasm and understanding of people, together with the fact that she had overcome secondary spread of breast cancer entirely by herself using a diet similar to that described in this book, were an inspiration to many of our patients. We were glad for her but sorry for our loss when she decided to remarry and left to live in the Lake District. There she now runs a support group for people following the 'Gentle Way' with cancer.

I have put Bea's story by itself in Appendix 3 because it is a superb example of how cancer can be tackled. It shows the refusal to give in, the persistence, the do-it-yourself attitude, the taking of responsibility for oneself and the originality that characterise those who do well on the 'Gentle Way'.

DIETARY HABITS

Dietary habits are not formed by instinct; they come more into the classification of desires. For example, if every time you cried as a child a sweet was stuffed into your mouth, you will have learned that the way to remain contented and not distressed tastes sweet. You may have been used to eating a lot of sugar and be developing a tendency to eat more and more. This happens because your taste buds soon become conditioned to moderate amounts of sugar and need more and more to stimulate them.

People can become sugarholics. The mechanism is simple; when you take sugar it is rapidly absorbed into the bloodstream and the sugar level shoots up. The pancreas then reacts strongly to this and insulin is secreted. Insulin is necessary for the entry of sugar into cells for storage or burning. The sugar level bounces down but, because there is always a delay in such a mechanism, the insulin goes on being produced for a little while. The sugar level then falls lower, and you get the feelings of hypoglycaemia – you feel hungry, uncomfortable, and perhaps a little sweaty or shaky if you respond in an extreme way to such low sugar levels. So you feel a craving for another dose of sugar, and so it goes on through the day. Sugarholics proceed from one sweet thing to another and, when it's an addictive thing like coffee, the sugarholic habit is reinforced strongly.

Some experimenters once tried to find a way of making rats fat in order to study obesity. They gave the rats good conditions, i.e. plenty of space and plenty of freely available high-quality rat food, but also provided the rats with a display of rich supermarket food. They found that the rats went straight for the supermarket food. The rats got a taste for sugar and sweet things and, in no time at all, the cages were full of fat rats swimming in the sawdust, paddling their way on their bellies towards the supermarket food because they were now so fat they could no longer walk. The same principle applies to animals as to humans – if the food tastes nice and is strongly flavoured, they become addicted to it. Since I learned about this experiment I have always noticed the fatties in the supermarkets congregating around the shelves with the sweet stuff on Saturday mornings.

So don't be confused about the diet. Look at it like this – ask yourself how far removed your regular food is from its natural state. Remember that the best thing you can do is to eat organically grown food that was harvested a short while ago and which hasn't been cooked. Achieving this is almost impossible in this country at present, but bear it in mind when you catch yourself thinking that a tin of peas would be 'just as good'.

HOW TO START ON THE DIET

Some people start by diving in at the deep end, making a sudden change in their diet, and they never look back; these are the lucky ones. For most people a slow start is much better. Take one of the meals in the day (the easiest is breakfast) and make that the first one you take which is totally according to the Get Well Diet (see Chapter 6). Well-soaked, prepared muesli doesn't taste too different from porridge. It can be sweetened slightly with raisins and perhaps a little honey and made with soya bean milk, though personally I use water now as it is much cheaper. I have used fruit juice in the past but I gave this up because the quality of fruit juices varies. Also, boxed juices can be expensive and many boxes are aluminium-lined which is not a good thing. In fact muesli prepared by overnight soaking in spring water has a purity of flavour which is, I now think, superior to the other methods. Once you have established one meal, go on to another meal. If you do this slowly, within a month your body will have accustomed itself to the new diet.

One thing needs to be made clear – this diet is not meant to be a punishment or a penance. If it starts to feel like that, and if it is all too much for you to cope with, then much of the point has been lost. Feeling fed-up with it all is understandable; but if you feel a guilty failure just because you can't stick it, then the situation must be reassessed. Perhaps you are not cooking things properly because you haven't learned how – so try a new way of cooking. All this takes time to learn, and your family may not be enthusiastic about the new diet. Ask them to help you to go on it. Many families all convert to the diet as they work on it together. Get some vegetarian cookbooks which tell you how to prepare tastier dishes. The recipe section of this book is designed to help with this, but you may find that the books listed on p. 171 are also helpful.

Feeling depressed and worried will do you more harm than backsliding on your diet. In a period of stress people tend to over-react to things. Hard though it may be to change your life in this way, try to stick to the diet, but keep a sense of proportion about everything. Have a good laugh at some of the difficulties; a sense of humour is very helpful here. Another sustaining thought is that you don't have to go on like this for ever. After three months you can begin to slack off the diet and reintroduce more cooked foods and so on, if you want to.

THE EFFECTS OF THE DIET

Many people start to feel better on this diet after only a short time. Some people who have taken a lot of additives in their food and eaten a bad diet for many years, and especially those who have had chemotherapy or have been heavy smokers, may feel somewhat sick and tired. They may also get the symptoms of overdosage of chemotherapy or of smoking. This is because the effect of the raw vegetable diet is to mobilise the poisons and force them out into the circulation so that they can be excreted. This is when you may need some liver stimulation. The simplest way to do this is to take some liver-stimulating herbs and any herbalist will help you with this.

Another method used by some therapists is the coffee enema, but this seems to me a somewhat drastic way of tackling a simple problem. Coffee is not a desirable part of any diet. It contains carcinogens; it contains a constrictor of the coronary arteries; it contains caffeine (a stimulant which some people think is not good for the kidneys either and which is somewhat addictive); and it uses up a lot of vitamin C. When given by mouth it tends to make the exit of the stomach contract, and that tends to shut off the flow of bile it produces. Given as an enema which is absorbed during 15 minutes and then released, it doesn't have the contracting effect on the outlet to the stomach and is a strong liver stimulant, but in practice I have found that the liver herbs seem to work with less trouble for the patient.

The above warning has been issued to let people who are sick know what to expect. The process goes on for only about a month and tends to come in waves which are produced by a build-up of toxins due to the liver's inability to cope with more than a certain load. The diet should be persisted with because, in about six weeks, you will feel very much better and will have got rid of most of the poisons that have accumulated in your body over the years.

People who are using this diet solely as a preventive measure do not usually have these symptoms and improvement is noticeable almost from the start.

SOME DIFFICULTIES

Obesity

Some people who tend to be overweight will gradually lose weight on the diet and then level out at their normal weight. Some people lose their appetite because of the struggle with dietary habits and don't eat enough; these lose a lot of weight. The way around this is to realise that you are not eating enough and to change your strategy. For instance, one person was losing weight rapidly, but she was taking only two dessertspoonfuls of muesli – she could have had ten times that amount. So if you are losing too much weight, take a lot more muesli, twice a day if necessary. Another thing that helps people who are not feeling well to put on weight is to eat more bananas.

If you are thin already there is no need to lose weight on this diet, but you have to eat enough food to avoid weight loss and it may be more than you are accustomed to if you are not feeling well. So bear this in mind; you may have to push yourself to maintain your correct weight.

People who have abdominal growths or colostomies

Most of these people do have some difficulty with the diet, though surprisingly some seem to have no trouble at all. If there are difficulties in swallowing, the diet should be liquidised and consumed as a thick soup.

If you have abdominal troubles and chewing up the food makes you feel tired, chop it up much finer or liquidise it. (A good food processor is a very useful tool.) It is also a good idea to make your dietary changes more gradual; take about six weeks making the changeover, but you must go on for eight weeks afterwards so it all takes longer.

For people with a colostomy much of what has been mentioned above applies, but you may also have to cut out certain foods that upset you (things like the cabbage family may stimulate you too much). A proportion of the raw vegetables may have to be cooked if they have too much of a stimulating effect on your remaining bowel. However, I have found that most people with a colostomy can manage our diet all right if they proceed gradually and bear in mind what has been said above.

Diarrhoea

For people who have suffered from constipation the Get Well Diet is good news. Most people have an increased bowel action and open their bowels several times a day; some remain a bit loose. If diarrhoea is a great problem the use of Fuller's Earth, which is rather better than kaolin, will help to steady your bowels. Mix the Fuller's Earth to a creamy consistency with water and take a dessertspoonful as a test dose; then vary from one to six dessertspoonfuls according to your needs.

6
THE
GET WELL DIET

SUMMARY

The Get Well Diet is:
A solid juice fast
Totally vegetable (vegan)
90 per cent raw food
Strictly salt free

With each meal have one of the items from the following list:
Buckwheat
Wholemeal bread
Wholegrain rice
Wholegrain millet
Wholegrain muesli

Drink water, herb teas or fresh pressed fruit juices.

Extra wholegrain cereals, such as muesli or rice, and bananas may be added if weight loss continues after six weeks.

Select food only from the list in Appendix I that is marked with two, three or four asterisks.

Eat slowly, in a relaxed manner, in pleasant surroundings; chew thoroughly.

SUGAR – DON'T EAT IT

That's really all there is to say. Sugar means not only the white form, but also all forms of brown sugar, molasses, glucose and honey. It is hard to give up the habit of a lifetime during which some people have become physically addicted to it – sugarholics in fact. Everything unnaturally sweet is unhealthy so do not add sugar to food or drink; avoid sweets, biscuits, cakes, custard, puddings, jams and marmalade.

Use no artificial sweeteners or artificially sweetened (diabetic) food or drink. There is possibly a connection between large amounts of saccharine and cancer. You can eat fresh fruit when on the Get Well Diet, though not in large quantities. Permission is only given for small amounts because, though these fruits contain sugar, they also contain the vitamins and minerals necessary to metabolise it.

Another important aspect when you eat solid, unprepared fresh fruit is that the sugar is released relatively slowly from it. It therefore produces a slow rise of the blood sugar level which gives a slow gentle stimulus to the mechanism that produces insulin in order to keep the blood sugar at its normal level. Therefore the insulin excreted in response to the stimulus of the rise in glucose in the blood has been used up by the time the glucose level has returned to normal. If, however, juice is extracted from a fruit, the sugar is much more readily available and the blood glucose goes to a much higher level, which gives a stronger stimulus to insulin secretion and a larger amount is released from the pancreas. When the blood glucose level has returned to normal, this insulin remains left over, and so the glucose level continues to fall. The individual may then feel hungry, may get sweaty and shaky, or even experience irrational changes in mood, and crave another sweet drink. So the process goes on with the blood sugar level swinging between extremes. Children who eat refined CHO get mild low blood sugar states frequently, the condition known as hypoglycaemia.

This is one of the mechanisms by which a person can be induced to eat too much refined CHO and therefore become too fat. Then when they have a lot of fat to support, more insulin is needed. This is because fat needs a constant supply of insulin to deal with the great amount of activity in fatty tissue. Eventually with the constant stimulation of the pancreas to produce more insulin in response to large amounts of sugar taken in and increasing obesity, the insulin-producing mechanism may reach its maximum capacity. A person in this position may become diabetic late in life. In some people there may be shortages of minerals and vitamins. This occurs in those who, in addition, do not eat a well-composed diet, which is very common. Fatigue, irritability and behaviour problems are common symptoms of such deficiencies.

SALT – DON'T ADD IT

One of the main aims of this diet is to reduce drastically the salt intake and increase the potassium intake. Salt has an addictive taste and once learned the salt eating habit can become quite strong – animals walk long distances to salt licks. In the average diet about 12 times more salt than is needed is taken. This tends to make us swollen because most of the sodium is in the fluid outside the cells. Potassium is mostly inside the cell and is needed for efficient cell function. If we eat a lot of processed food it may be in short supply, especially in summer. Too much sodium in the diet can even displace potassium from the cells which then do not function so well. Other troubles with salt are that it causes high blood pressure, and one of the factors which promotes cancer is a lack of potassium and an excess of sodium in the cells. Correcting this helps cancer.*

Meat needs salt to improve its taste. This is another reason for avoiding meat and the reason for eating lots of vegetables and grains – they have more potassium and little salt.

Take as little salt as possible. Sea salt has extra trace minerals so use that – but in the smallest quantities. Avoid purified salts that contain running agents, they are mildly poisonous. Get your iodine from kelp. Do not eat salted foods. All bought bread contains salt, so make it yourself.

SEEDS

Seeds are the main source of energy-giving starches and protein (see also Flour and Bread p. 84, and Protein p. 30). There are five sorts of seeds. The first – soya beans – are perfectly adequate, high-quality protein in themselves. The

* *A Cancer Therapy – Results of Fifty Cases*, Max Gerson MD, Totality Books, PO Box 1035, Del Mar, Cal. 92014 USA.

seeds in the other four categories (listed below) are not complete in themselves and therefore some of the first group (Grains and Cereals), plus one or two from the remaining three groups (Pulses, Nuts, and Small Seeds), should be taken at each meal. When these two or three types of vegetable protein are eaten together, they combine to form a high-quality protein that supplies all the essential amino-acids.

Grains and Cereals

These come from grasses – wheat, oats, barley, rye, millet, maize and rice. All should be eaten whole, though they may be cracked (as in bulgar from wheat), rolled (usually as oats, barley or millet), ground into flour (wheat, maize, rice and rye) or sprouted. Usually only wheat is sprouted making a berry which goes well in salads and also cooked with rice; the others do not make useful sprouts. The wheat berries should be eaten young otherwise, like the other grains, they get stringy rapidly. Eat them before roots and leaves develop, while the single sprout is short. Wholegrain rice is often called brown rice. Maize flour is called polenta in Italy and this is a commonly used name. Soya bean flour is also available.

Some people are gluten-sensitive. They should avoid wheat, oats, barley and rye. Since so-called gluten-free flour may contain up to 2 per cent gluten, it is best for those who are gluten-sensitive to omit these four grains entirely from their diet and use other flours, e.g. soya flour, and buckwheat flour which can be made by grinding dry buckwheat in a mortar – it powders easily. People who are gluten-sensitive should read a book called *Good Food – Gluten Free*.* Sprouting breaks down the gluten in wheat so wheat berries are allowable to otherwise wheat-sensitive people.

Cereals are eaten as *bread* (wheat and rye – see pp. 84–7), or *boiled* (millet, buckwheat, oats – as porridge, cracked wheat and rice), or *rolled* into flakes which can be taken dry, soaked with water as muesli, or boiled as puddings or porridge, or as *sprouts*.

* *Good Food – Gluten Free* by Cherry Hills, published by Roberts Publications, 225 Putney Bridge Road, London SW15 2PY.

Pulses

Pulses are the seeds of pea and bean plants such as: lentils (small, large, yellow, orange, brown or green), peas (green and chick), beans (black, white, red, brown, broad, lima, kidney, black-eyed susan, aduki, mung and soya).

Pulses are eaten as sprouts or, after soaking and slow boiling, baked (often with onion, garlic and tomato). They are inclined to give people wind, especially the beans, so avoid large helpings if this bothers you. It is harmless though uncomfortable; don't bottle it up out of a sense of shyness – go somewhere private and relieve yourself of it frequently. As mentioned above, soya beans are also made into flour.

Nuts

Nuts are the seeds of trees: hazel, almonds, walnuts, brazils, pecans, cashews, pistachios, pine kernels, prune and apricot kernels. They can be eaten raw, alone or in salads, baked or boiled.

Brazil nuts contain a lot of methionine which is a relatively scarce amino-acid, but many people are allergic to these nuts so I would advise caution in eating them. An additional disadvantage is that nowadays most of them are free of their very hard shells and the brown skin which coats them has mostly been torn off during the preparation. Therefore they are liable to be rancid and have their essential fats damaged and turned into carcinogens by oxidation before they are eaten.

Pistachio nuts only really taste nice if they are split and heavily salted. For this reason they should not be eaten except in the Stay Well stage; they have no place in the Get Well Diet.

Peanuts are not a proper nut because they grow underground, but they look more like a nut than a seed. Growing in the ground and having to be dug out makes them liable to contamination with fungi which can be poisonous. When ground up, as butter, they mostly contain emulsifiers. When bought roasted they are coated with extra salt and artificial flavourings, so they are to be avoided. Cooked peanuts don't taste particularly good. But, when roasted by yourself and then ground up, they can make good stews. However, on the whole for the above reasons they are not particularly recommended.

Small Seeds

Small seeds are from various plants such as pumpkins (good for the prostate gland in men), sunflower, sesame, flax, linseed or buckwheat, alfalfa, fenugreek and rape. Many of these smaller seeds can be sprouted (see section on Sprouting pp. 140–41) or roasted and ground.

FLOUR AND BREAD

Flour and bread are perfect examples of how legislation intended to preserve our health does nothing of the sort. Bread has always been regarded as an important staple item of food. Since the Middle Ages there has been legislation to improve its quality and prevent dilution of the flour with various additives, but even with the advances of science in the last hundred years and the later stimulus of two world wars the situation is still very unsatisfactory. Dr Kenneth Arnold in *The Law and the Loaf* (Precision Press, 1978) has dealt with this aspect thoroughly, and so has Miriam Polunin in *The Right Way to Eat* (Dent, 1978).

It seems that wherever there is a staple food that is widely produced throughout the world there are three things that you can be sure about. The first is that the producer will get the lowest possible profit from his hard work. In recent years, however, there has been a tendency to overproduce wheat in the United States and the farmers there do get generous subsidies for their production, but the motive is political. The second is that the consumer's needs as regards taste and nutritional value get scant consideration. The third thing that you can be sure about is that the legislation regulating the production of this food will not be adequate and will favour commercial interests rather than those of health.

The sad tale about flour and bread starts with the methods of agriculture used on the soil that produces it. Where there is good wheat land, wheat tends to be the sole product. There is no mixed agriculture. Enormous wheat fields have been made in order to make reaping easier by mechanical means. The soil is slowly exhausted because there is not enough cattle manure available to put humus back into it; essential nutrients are gradually used up and are only partially replaced by artificial fertilisers which increase the production rate at the expense of quality.

Next, the storage of the wheat is inadequate. It is kept in too damp conditions. Moulds enter into the wheat and grow. It has not yet been fully realised how important these moulds may be to health.

The flour is repeatedly ground between rollers and sifted until it has been divided neatly into four parts: animal fodder (i.e. much of the proteins, vitamins and minerals); the wheatgerm with vitamin E particularly and many other vitamins; bran; and white flour. After this some of the iron is put back; powdered chalk is added, which raises the calcium to about four and a half times that in the original flour; and some nicotinic acid (for vitamin B3) and thiamine (vitamin B1) are added which brings the content up to about one-third of the original level of the latter two vitamins. These additives are compulsory by law. If it wasn't for this, bread would be very deficient. Even so, it loses most of the pyridoxine (vitamin B6), half the pantothenic acid (vitamin B5) and molybdenum, nearly all the vitamin E, cobalt and zinc, and about 50 per cent of the chromium and 15 per cent of the selenium which is in short supply anyhow in English soil.

The degradation of the nutritional content of the wheat is continued with the addition of bleaches and improvers. Chlorine dioxide and chlorine came into use in the early 1950s to replace agene. This flour bleacher and 'improver' was banned in 1950 after it had been shown to produce fits in animals. Agene also contains chlorine. It is nitrogen trichloride. A commonly-used basic bleaching agent is benzoyl peroxide. This is an explosive substance which is used for external application only in acne because it erodes the skin. It can cause dermatitis. The *Extra Pharmacopoeia* does not recommend it to be taken internally. Another additive which is always present in white flour, because it reduces the time of kneading by increasing its elasticity, is potassium bromate. This is definitely poisonous. Many cases of bromate poisoning are recorded. There is a report of bromate poisoning in 816 people who had eaten bread baked from dough containing an excessive amount of potassium bromate added as a flour improver. The bread contained 1.1 per cent instead of a permitted 40 parts per million. Deafness, renal failure, fits, severe abdominal pain, diarrhoea, hepatitis, pulmonary oedema and toxic myocarditis have also been reported due to its use.*

The only flour which is safe from these things is wholewheat flour that is guaranteed stone-ground and free from such additives. With the increasing popularity of wholewheat flour it is highly likely that bakers will be pressing the millers to put improvers and such substances as those mentioned above, of which there are many more, into wholemeal flour so that they can manipulate it more easily.

The health magazine *Here's Health* has done spot checks of over 60 loaves from different towns and different bakers' shops and analysed them for their fibre content. These were definitely sold as wholemeal or wholewheat. Their tests have shown that half of these loaves were not wholemeal because their fibre content was too low. A wholemeal loaf is expected to have at least 1.8 per cent fibre by dry weight. The loaves tested fell below this level. It is also possible that a number of loaves made of white flour to which bran had been added in exactly the right amount to give a 1.8 per cent fibre content could have been used and this would not have been shown up by the tests done by *Here's Health*. Therefore more than half may have been substandard.

There is another point to watch for when buying bread. Cut the loaf in half and look at it. If there is a circular arrangement of the air bubbles in the loaf, it has been prepared by machinery and is highly likely to contain plasticisers which make the process of kneading shorter and easier. Some of these loaves do not have much yeast in them. The rising is not natural – it is produced by injected air.

Once the wheat has been milled all the vitamins start to deteriorate because they are active chemical substances and

* Martingdale, The *Extra Pharmacopoeia* (The Pharmaceutical Press, 1977).

easily oxidised. So by the time bread comes to be made from the wholemeal its vitamin content will have been reduced much further than when it was freshly milled.

The only way you can have a safe loaf is to buy wheat that has been grown from soil manured by compost without any sprays. It should be freshly grown that year and you should buy it as soon after the harvest as possible and keep it dry. Then grind it just before you make the bread. This is the only way you can be sure that what you are getting is a pure product. Many small bakers start off in this way and their bread is so good that it is readily bought, and demand increases. Soon the baker's production capacity is overwhelmed and he has to increase his production and use machinery. After that the quality of the bread deteriorates. The machinery usually needs a large volume of dough and is also designed to use plasticated dough. The baker has problems letting the yeast rise and so forth, because time factors demand quick rising, and so he has to adopt the use of additives.

The only acceptable dodge commercial bakers use is to add vitamin C to the dough. Ascorbic acid (vitamin C) is helpful in speeding up the fermentation of the dough so that not much kneading is required and it rises quickly. As vitamin C is a natural product, and our intake of it tends to be a bit short, I think this is a safe and useful practice. I use it myself but, because bread making takes a lot of time and I am busy, I have practically given up eating bread. My grain intake comes from eating a lot of muesli which has a much wider range of sources of grain and seeds so one gets more vitamins and minerals that way, especially if the muesli is allowed to sprout a little by being soaked overnight.

Naturally, all scones, pancakes, rolls, cakes, biscuits, and so on are forbidden unless made without sugar and with wholemeal. Macaroni and spaghetti are usually made from white flour. However, in health-food stores, and increasingly in supermarkets, you can buy these made from wholewheat meal or buckwheat. Check the packet to make sure there are no additives or preservatives and as a precaution it is worthwhile, if you are very keen on purity, to write to the manufacturers to get their assurance on this point.

The Average British Diet

As an example of the sort of thing that happens between the food industry and the government let us take the two-year-old report of the National Advisory Committee on Nutrition Education. The publication of this has been held up because of opposition from the food industry. The scientific basis of the report is sound and its dietary recommendations moderate. It says the average British diet is a major cause of many of the diseases we suffer. This is news the public need to have. But it could mean major changes to Britain's agriculture and food processing industry.

. . . both the British Nutrition Foundation and the Food and Drinks Industries Council have opposed the report.

The British Nutrition Foundation is an independent body and is declared so in its statute. Its current chairman Dr Alan Robertson stresses that the foundation is able to work successfully and efficiently without interference. That work includes, a spokesman said, providing an information service to the public, sponsoring research and publishing a nutrition magazine.

Yet 98 per cent of the funding of the foundation comes from the food industry in the form of members' fees. Almost all the major household names in the food industry such as Tate & Lyle, Rowntrees, Cadbury's, Kelloggs, Weetabix, Whitworths are members. Payments and the scale of fees are based on turnover of the company.

'The foundation seeks to broaden the level of knowledge about nutrition', said a spokesman. 'We remain sceptical about the report.'

The British Sugar Bureau, the sugar industry's main lobby organisation which is known to have a powerful voice at Westminster doesn't accept the report – because officially it doesn't exist.

The Dairy Council said the nutritional claims made in the report represented only some of the views of nutritionists and the council had to view 'the total picture'. A spokesman said that there had been a lot of publicity about the report but until it became official it was premature to comment. *

* *Here's Health*, September 1983.

This summer the Health Education Council has been making the report available as a 'discussion document' to those professionally concerned with health and nutrition education.

FATS AND OILS

In Southern Italy farmers put the best of the olives into circular stone troughs with a heavy roller in a groove. The best oil that just oozes from the olives is scooped off and kept as food for young children. The oil that is pressed is called the virgin oil and kept for adult consumption locally. The mash of olives is then sold with the medium olives for the production of commercial table oil. This is done by the cold-pressing process in a screw expeller from which the oil comes out at about 100°C – not so cold as you would think. The residue from this process and the dud olives are sold on for solvent or super-heated steam extraction. So there is more to good oil than just cold-pressed and hot-pressed.

The usual cooking oil is extracted by grinding the basic material (seeds, nuts or beans), steaming and mixing with petroleum-based solvents which may be carcinogenic. After evaporating the solvent the extracted oil is washed with caustic soda, bleached and deodorised. Thus the oil's natural anti-oxidants have been destroyed and chemical antioxidants are added. By this method the delicate essential fatty acids have disappeared and carcinogens are present.

Fat intake should be kept as low as possible. For salad dressings use cold-pressed sunflower oil or olive oil if you like the taste. For cooking avoid butter – it gets burnt. Ghee (see p. 141) is better. It is salt-free butter changed by heating and skimming. This removes the proteins, unstable fats and water which help butter to go rancid, so it keeps well. It also gives a buttery flavour to food and does not burn.

It is preferable to margarine which is oil that has gone through even more processing than cooking oil and is made from lower grade oils, sometimes from worn out deep-frying oil which contains carcinogens. Margarine sometimes contains added vitamin D which can accumulate and cause an overdose of the vitamin, leading to a high blood calcium. This can cause dangerous deposits of calcium in the organs and damage kidneys.

When buying butter, choose one that is pale and whiteish. It may not look so nice, but you can be fairly sure that it has no artificial colouring material in it. Denmark has the strictest laws about freshness and adulteration of dairy products in the EEC.

To convert essential fatty acids into nervous tissue and prostaglandins (chemical messengers) the body has a limited amount of one enzyme. If too much fat that is *not* essential is eaten, the enzyme is used up in getting this fat stored or burnt and is then not available for the important process of converting the essential fatty acids. So keep your fat and oil intake down. No butter on bread or toast, except occasionally for treats when you are well again.

A test for rancidity

An oil is rancid if it throws a white deposit when kept in a refrigerator. This test shows when an oil has become too oxidised and has gone off long before it can be detected by taste.

VEGETABLES

Appendix 1 lists vegetables graded into different degrees of suitability. For the Get Well Diet use only those with two, three or four stars.

Some well-known vegetables receive a surprisingly low rating; this is not because they are chemically unsuitable but because they have a low rating according to another vitalistic system of therapy. For instance, tomatoes, peppers (red or green) and aubergines are of the deadly nightshade family as well as being very yin according to macrobiotic theory. Onions and garlic are not considered suitable for cancer patients by Tibetan medical practitioners. However, both are highly rated by all systems for their beneficial effects on infections and should be freely eaten by everyone who does not have cancer.

Cucumbers have a low rating because they are very yin fruit macrobiotically. Parsnips contain a carcinogen, psoralen, which vastly increases when the root is diseased; hence its low rating. Celery and parsley also contain some psoralens.

Much of the best part of most vegetables lies close under the skin. Wash them thoroughly and scrub, but do *not* scrape or peel them. Cut out any bad bits freely.

Eat as much as possible of your vegetable intake *raw* as salads; shred everything finely. The addition of some chopped nuts and sprouted grains will add protein and balance the dish. Dressings are to have very little oil – sunflower is a good one – and the sharpener can be lemon, orange or grapefruit juice. These are nicer than vinegar (cider or wine, not ordinary). Don't add extra salt and use the dressing sparingly. Mix the salad thoroughly; it makes the dressing go further. Yoghourt and juices make a good low fat dressing.

When vegetables are cooked they can be fried briefly in a hot pan thinly coated with oil so that they remain crisp. They should be kept moving. This preserves the vitamins and prevents carcinogens forming in the oil. There are two other ways of cooking vegetables to preserve their vitamin content as much as possible: one is to stew the vegetables on a very low heat without any water and just a trace of ghee in the pan to prevent sticking. The other way is to steam them lightly, leaving them half cooked by ordinary standards.

Make the most of your salads. They are the best food you can eat. Start the meal with a big helping of salad then take the CHO and protein part. This way gets the digestive juices working best.

If you have a sensitive stomach you may find it helpful *not* to mix fruit and vegetables at the same meal. This means that you don't have a fruit salad for dessert, but have it later at another meal such as breakfast. So you won't be able to eat a lot of fruit, but that's no bad thing as fruits have a high sugar content.

DRINKS

Drinks are to be taken about half an hour before food. This is because during a meal the outlet from the stomach shuts down, the gastric juices are secreted and start digesting the food, and the stomach gently churns the mixture. Drinking with the meal dilutes the digestive juices and slows their action. The stomach is also more distended because its outlet is closed for action. Normally a drink passes on fairly soon if the stomach is empty, unless it is iced. In that case the cold stimulates the outlet to close.

There are many herbal teas in most health food shops and, although at first they may seem rather obnoxious in comparison with the cup of tea or coffee that you have been used to, after a while you not only get used to them but feel very refreshed after drinking them. Search and you will find one you like. Tea and coffee are poisonous to the system, and glowing health is soon lost by those who drink these beverages. It makes good sense therefore to drink beverages that are beneficial to health.

It is not necessary to drink herbal teas if you find them completely unacceptable, but drink is essential for health so I have listed below ideas other than the carrot juice which is on p. 134.

Fresh spring water (where possible)
Apple juice
Berry juices (e.g. raspberry, blackcurrant, blackberry)
Citrus fruit juices
Grape juice
Watermelon juice
Pineapple juice
Prune juice
Coconut milk

These raw juice drinks will supply the daily requirement of vitamins to anyone whose digestion is very delicate in the initial stages of their treatment, but it is important to realise that raw salads are equally important for their enzyme content. These can also be liquidised if you feel too weak to cope at the beginning. At this point I would like to stress that one should try to progress a little at a time rather than get frustrated by becoming anxious and too ambitious. One strong step in the right direction is worth more than ten weak steps that end in one losing ground and losing faith.

A very small amount of alcohol, which must not be more than two glasses of good wine or two standard tots of spirits each day, will stimulate the production of prostaglandin E1 which is needed for the functioning of the immune system, so this amount will do you good. More than this is a sedative poison which depresses all body functions.

Slippery elm is a very comforting bedtime drink. Taken with a little soya milk and a teaspoon of honey it soothes the intestinal system and has a beneficial healing effect.

A PERSONAL EXPERIENCE OF THE GET WELL DIET – KATHY ARMSTRONG

I have worked in the kitchen preparing the diet for the Cancer Help Centre for two years and have come into close contact with the patients. Mostly they are interested in the variety of meals that can be produced as well as the flavourings we use. Their enquiries led me to produce some recipes for this book to give some inspiration to the flagging spirit. What struck me most was the patients' need to feel that their food was normal and that it was the rest of humanity that was to a great extent misguided in what they ate. My train of thought encouraged me to take a step that I had long felt the need of. This was to adopt the diet and experience the problems that the patients may have.

I am 43, not fat but well-covered, tall and most of the time look extremely healthy. I wish that I was built like a gazelle. Don't we all! After much reading, and encouraging the patients in their quest for better health, I was struck by the fact that, although I have always found time and energy for others, I have very rarely found time to concentrate on myself. In retrospect, I can say that I am extremely fortunate in not having cancer myself. One saving factor in my favour is my positive nature which, I can see now, has helped me through many difficult periods in my life. About a month ago I decided to go vegan vegetarian and to note the changes in myself for the benefit of the so-called well members of your families who feel they do not need this diet.

In the first part of the book Dr Forbes mentions the fact that some people need meat. Fortunately, I am not one of those, but I do like the gravies. I did manage to get hold of an extremely good vegan cookbook* which helped me on my way, and I do like to experiment. Also I am one of those people who believe in leading by example.

I have had circulation problems since childhood. Since changing my diet this has very much improved. After the winter I shall know more, although I used to be troubled even during the summer months.

My skin has become extremely silky, as if I have been oiled; the elbows and soles of the feet (little parts that show dry patches first) are also soft. My nails are stronger (no more brittle breaks). My hair is more manageable and in good condition. I am losing those little rolls of fat and my muscle tone has improved.

The best news is the cost. I have listened to a lot of people, not only patients, saying that they were put off by the cost. It's a fallacy. I was intent on trying the diet for myself and my husband on £20 per week for the two of us. I have done more than that – this amount includes other household items. It took me a week or so to build up different stocks of nuts and grains, but it is definitely cheaper than a conventional diet. I have taken into account the buying of what some might term exotic fruits and vegetables, just to vary the diet as much as possible, and I still come out with a plus.

I feel that it is important for everyone to realise that it is not just a question of food, but how much we care about what we eat. Knowing that my body is a temple, why should I want to treat it with disrespect by allowing rubbish to enter it. I have had to make a real effort to love myself the way I readily give my love to others, to slow down and to take time to make sure that I enjoy my food.

* Any vegan cookbook will do but its recipes must be modified to the Bristol Diet standards set out in this book.

7
THE
STAY WELL DIET

SUMMARY

Follow the Get Well Diet with the following additions:

One-star items in Appendix 1 may be added.
Three eggs and not more than 1lb (450g) of fish and fowl are allowed per week. If you do not have cancer, lean meat can be included.
More cooked vegetables may be taken, but eat 50 per cent as raw fresh vegetables.
An occasional treat is permitted once a fortnight.
A teaspoon of honey may be used for sweetening drinks..

Don't be like the fat man who said, 'Honey is good for you, isn't it?'

'Yes,' I said cautiously, 'it's the most nutritious form of sugar. How much do you eat a week?'

'Two pounds', was the reply.

Remember the phrase the Greeks used to put up in their temples, 'Nothing too much'; another was 'Know thyself'. Don't go back to being a sugarholic. A lot of what you fancy kills you slowly.

You can now have tomatoes, mushrooms and peppers in salads. Mushrooms are quite a good source of vitamin D, a lot of B-group vitamins, and minerals, especially iron. Yoghourt can be taken more often if you are well. It will help to increase the intake of calcium and vitamin D. In yoghourt the milk sugar is turned into lactic acid, the protein digested and the growth of the right bacteria in the intestine encouraged; it has many advantages. Do not buy supermarket yoghourt – only the sort freshly made from boiled milk. It is best to make it yourself (see p. 133).

An occasional potato will not be harmful, eaten whole when new, and baked in the skin when old – eat the skin too. It is only the skin and the part just under it that are of any value. Possibly with the potato comes the moment for an occasional treat of a dab of real butter, but don't do this more than once a fortnight. Turnips and swedes, but not parsnips, are allowed and make for variety.

If you go out and are served meat, and don't want to make a fuss, eat the gravy; take large helpings of the vegetables. If you go to a restaurant it is simple to order fish or an omelette.

MODIFICATIONS FOR CANCER

You should always be careful of your diet if you have recovered from cancer. Don't let up too soon. If you have had apparently successful treatment and are following The Gentle Way, stay on the Get Well Diet for at least six months. That is the minimum time it takes for the body to recover from the years of neglect. It would be better to stay on this diet for more than a year.

Always eat more than an average amount of carrots. If you have decided to go back to eating flesh, be careful to avoid those types liable to pollution. Choose deep-sea fish like cod and avoid flat fish, mackerel, pollock, shellfish and rock fish, etc. Avoid beef, for the cow is now one of the most medicated of animals. Drenched and injected all its life, it cannot wash its food free of weedkillers nor stop its drinking water and grass being heavily polluted with nitrates.

Milk and cheese, unless made from boiled milk, contain the growth factor which stimulates cancer cells. Cottage-type cheeses tend to form complexes with zinc that prevent its absorption. Cream cheeses and hard cheeses that have been concentrated are rich in fat and salt. Both milk and cheese are considered by Eastern systems of medicine to increase the formation of mucus. My personal and professional experience agrees with this view. Therefore they are out in the active stage of cancer and only for rare treats thereafter.

Carrots have been shown to prevent cancer,* so a large intake and even a daily glass of emulsified carrot juice would be helpful. Carotene neutralises a muco-protein that surrounds cancer and dissolves in the blood, blocking the action of the cells which seek out and eat cancer cells. Dissolving the carotene in the carrot juice with oil by emulsifying it in a liquidiser greatly improves its absorption by the lymphatic system. This means that it bypasses the liver and is therefore not stored by that organ before it has had a chance to circulate in the blood and neutralise the immunity-blocking muco-protein.

Having a fairly high vitamin C intake is also a precaution that seems promising. The great apes, who are of similar size and biochemical constitution to humans, do not last long in captivity unless they receive a daily supplement of 1,000mg. Without this amount they die of common human diseases such as cancer, hardening of the arteries, ulcers and pneumonia. The same dose would seem indicated for people who have recovered from cancer.

Selenium and zinc would also seem to be worthwhile daily supplements to keep up indefinitely for the reasons given in Chapter 4. Tablets of 200µg of selenium as an organic compound in a selenium yeast and of 15mg of zinc orotate, that supply the average daily requirement in one dose of each metal, are recommended.

MODIFICATIONS FOR OTHER CONDITIONS

If you are healthy and have gone through three months on the Get Well Diet you need make no modifications to the Stay Well Diet. Try to make this what you enjoy. You can have a little more salt, but remember it is addictive. You can have red meat occasionally for treats, but remember it is polluted. Communicate with your body, ask it to tell you how it feels. If it gives you back a pleasant vibrant or tingling sensation and you feel alive and vigorous you are healthy. There may be a few areas of disease in your body, but you are in harmony with them and

* Editorial, 'Vitamin A and Cancer', *BMJ*, vol. 281 (1980), p. 957.

are well. Everybody over 50 has at least three disease processes present in their bodies. This is normal. We are all going to die of some condition some time. Accept this, but don't worry about it. Enjoy each moment. Life is a valuable process of learning. Love living. Love your body; it is your closest neighbour – far closer than the people next door.

For *obesity* occasional juice fasts are the easiest way of getting trim quickly and are perfectly safe. You don't have to go to a health farm to do them and you need not stop working. Read more about fasts in Paavo Airola's book.*

Atheroma (arteriosclerosis, hardening of the arteries) results in coronary heart disease, strokes and poor circulation of the legs and hands. In this condition there should be emphasis on a low visible fat intake (see Chapter 4, pp. 35–9). Chromium, vitamin B6, selenium and vitamin E deficiency play a part in the production of atheroma. Large amounts of brewers' yeast help with the first two; selenium needs a special sort of yeast tablet (see under Modifications for Cancer); and plenty of wheatgerm helps to make up vitamin E. Larger amounts of this vitamin can be taken in capsules; a total of 800 to 1,200mg a day is recommended by several experts. Be careful to have your blood pressure checked if there is a tendency for this to be raised (in a few people vitamin E puts it up).

In *multiple sclerosis* a gluten-free diet is worth a trial (see p. 82). Strict attention should be given to keeping the visible fat intake as low as you can, and possible blocks in the conversion of linoleic acid into linolenic acid can be bypassed by taking Evening Primrose oil (see Fats, in Chapter 4). Supplements of zinc, vitamins B6 and C should also be taken (see the previous sections of this chapter). Some herbalists also recommend liver-regenerating herbs.

Many so-called *allergies* are either only failures of badly nourished cells to resist poisons in the diet or environment, are due to hypoglycaemia, vitamin or mineral deficiencies, or are physical responses to negative emotions or stress. True allergies caused by sensitisation of the immune system to foreign

* *How to Keep Slim, Healthy & Young with Juice Fasting* by Paavo Airola, Health Plus Publications, PO Box 22001, Phoenix, Arizona 85028, USA.

substances that have entered the body are rarer, but still common. Following the Get Well–Stay Well Diet sequence or making the appropriate psychological adjustments are the ways of getting rid of the first five types of so-called allergies. For true allergies, avoidance of the offending agent is the simplest way. This is best discovered by carefully observing what makes the allergic symptom worse. Then do several bouts of abstinence, followed by a challenge, to see if you are right. Tests for allergies give too many false positive results. Everybody is slightly allergic to many things but they don't produce symptoms or only do so when the person is very upset. A juice fast to get rid of the symptom followed by adding a new item of food every day until the symptom returns takes too long for most people. Other ways of sorting out allergies need a specialist allergy unit to work out the problem. Dr Richard Mackarness has written two helpful books on this subject.*

AN ALTERNATIVE SYSTEM

Macrobiotics is the name given to the application of the principles of Far Eastern medicine to diet. Every foodstuff is classified on a scale between the two extremes of yin (expansion) and yang (contraction). These are invisible, non-physical energies that are modifications of another higher energy called Ch'i (pronounced kee). This is an extreme simplification of the subject. A healthy diet is evenly balanced so that it is neither yin nor yang. Some diseases are considered to be due to excess of yin food or lifestyle and others to be due to excess of yang food or lifestyle. This sounds complicated but, once the many characteristics of yin and yang are learnt and understood, one is in possession of a simple practical way of understanding diets, diseases and lifestyles. No expensive investigations are needed.

Cancers are of two types in this system, yin or yang. Eating the opposite sort of diet to the type of cancer restores the state of sick person to normal. Michio Kushi, the main teacher of this system in the West, has recently published an excellent

* *Not All in the Mind* and *Chemical Victims* by R. Mackarness (Pan).

book on the subject and we will certainly be exploring its use in the future. (See Suggested Reading.)

PREVENTION

It only requires me to point out again the old saying 'Prevention is better than cure', and to state that it is nearly too late to give up sacrificing principles to expediency. The best use of the Get Well and Stay Well diets is for prevention.

8
RECIPES
AND MENUS

Here are some recipes and suggestions for a week's menus. If you want to make adjustments according to your tastes, then do so, but remember:

1. You must stop eating the things which your body has to work hard to deal with, and are full of useless or even dangerous matter which has to be eliminated, and

2. You must start eating foods which are positively beneficial to the body, and will bolster its attempts to rid itself of disease.

BREAKFAST SUGGESTIONS

Breakfast is the most important meal of the day; we have fasted for maybe eight hours. Care should be taken to allow sufficient time not only to prepare, but to eat, by chewing the food thoroughly to activate the saliva, which will help digestion in the stomach. All drinks should be taken at least half an hour before eating.

The following are just ten examples of nourishing easy-to-prepare breakfasts for any of the family.

1. Cooked cereal (steamed if possible) with chopped dates. (See recipe below.)

2. Crushed banana mixed with sunflower seeds (as they are or ground in the blender) on toast or wholemeal bread.

3. Melon: scoop out the seeds and fill the cavity with slices of banana, chopped nuts and sultanas; sprinkle with nutmeg (freshly ground) if desired. Charentais melons are especially good for this dish, one half will more than fill the 'big eater'.

4. Bulgar wheat soaked overnight in apple juice, served with fresh or dried fruits.
5. Stewed prunes with a little honey to taste.
6. Peanut, seed and honey spread – with toast or plain wholemeal bread.
7. Avocado and banana slices sprinkled with sesame seeds.
8. Raisins soaked in hot water for a few minutes to soften, put into blender with coconut (creamed, from a packet, or desiccated or grated fresh coconut with the milk). To sharpen, add some fresh lemon juice, or orange juice.
9. Couscous soaked for an hour or so until soft. Add sultanas and some fresh fruit as the season permits.
10. Muesli soaked in either apple juice or soya milk or, for a treat, some goat's yoghourt. (See recipe below.)

Cooked Cereal

Soak overnight:

½ tbs of whole buckwheat	½ tbs of whole millet
½ tbs of flaked oats (Jumbo oats)	½ tbs flaked wheat, barley or rye

Simmer over low heat until desired consistency (additional water may be added) 5–10 minutes. Eat with fresh fruit and a little yoghourt.

Muesli

Do not buy ready mixed muesli. It is usually pre-cooked with added sugar and milk powder. Use an organically grown muesli base with as many different grains as possible. Add some roughly crushed buckwheat, sesame seeds, sunflower seeds and wheatgerm (which must be kept in the fridge), some raisins, currants and half a level teaspoonful of kelp powder, and add water until the grain is just awash. Leave this to soak overnight in a warm place. In the morning or when the dish is required, add grated almonds, brazils, hazel nuts and pumpkin seeds and a little fruit juice, and some fresh fruit in season. Soya milk and a little honey can also be added. Crushed millet and linseed may also be added.

SALADS

Thoroughly wash the vegetables, but do not scrape or peel them if you can avoid it. Most of the goodness is usually found in the skins. You could mix all kinds of vegetables grated finely in a bowl and eat them together, or you may find it more satisfying to keep all greens and root vegetables apart and make separate salads of them.

Coleslaw

225g (½lb) hard cabbage	1 medium carrot
1 medium apple	1 medium onion

Shred the above finely, mix together and dress with the following:

1 dsp oil	1 sprig of borage or parsley,
2 tsp lemon juice or	chopped
cider vinegar	2 comfrey leaves (chopped)

Add a little more water or lemon juice as required or use yoghourt dressing for a change.

Red Cabbage and Orange Salad

225g (½lb) red cabbage	1 orange

Chop cabbage finely, add some chives, parsley, and the zest from the orange. Mix well with half the orange, peeled and chopped, and dress with the juice from the other half.

Sprouted Alfalfa Salad

2 tbs sprouted alfalfa	1 medium carrot, grated
1 tsp chopped chives	½ bunch watercress,
	chopped

Mix together and dress with a little lemon and oil dressing.

Dandelion Salad

1 good handful of young and tender dandelion leaves, chopped
few spring onions or chives, chopped

½ bunch watercress, chopped
1 tbs parsley, chopped

Mix together and serve with lemon and oil dressing.

Spanish Salad

1 onion, thinly sliced
some chicory, chopped
1 tsp chopped mint

1 orange in slices and chopped
a little lettuce, shredded

Mix together, with a dressing if preferred, and serve on lettuce leaves.

Sweet Potato Salad

450g (1lb) sweet potatoes, boil and chop into squares or slice

While still warm pour over the following dressing:

2 tsp oil
1 medium onion, finely chopped

1 tbs lemon juice or cider vinegar
1 clove garlic, crushed (if liked)

Mix this well with the sweet potatoes and cool, serve sprinkled with parsley or lemon balm.

Winter Salad

Lettuce, chopped
1 medium carrot, grated

Celery, chopped
½ beetroot, grated

Mix together with a dressing and serve on lettuce leaves with chopped watercress.

Fennel Salad

1 good sized fennel bulb	**1 large eating apple or orange**

Wash, slice and mix together. Dress with a little lemon juice and serve on a bed of shredded cabbage or spinach leaves.

Stuffed Pear Salad

½ ripe dessert pear	**½ avocado**
a little lemon juice	**a little ginger**
2 tsp sunflower seeds	

Brush pear with lemon juice. Mash avocado with lemon juice, ginger and sunflower seeds, pile into pear and decorate with a few grapes, if you have them.

Mixed Salad

Take quantities as required and mix: Chinese leaves, lettuce, thinly sliced Jerusalem artichokes, sunflower seeds or sunflower seed sprouts, spring onions, chopped marrow or courgette. Add lemon and oil dressing quickly to stop artichokes from discolouring.

Runner Bean Salad

Try this and see if you like it:

2–3 runner beans, sliced	**a little shredded cabbage**
1 stick celery, chopped	**chopped onion to taste**

Add oil and vinegar dressing, or avocado and cashew dressing.

Carrot and Orange Salad

Grate 2 carrots	**peel and chop 1 orange**

Mix together with a little of the zest of the orange and 2–3 dsp of orange juice. Try adding a little onion.

Beetroot and Apple Salad

Grate finely 1 beetroot and 1 apple, the proportions to be about ½–½. A little cumin or caraway seed (soaked for 1 hour in warm water before using) may be added to give extra taste, or try a little grated onion and carrot. Also a little grated fresh horseradish or ginger, if liked, adds variety.

Fresh Spinach Salad

Wash and chop 1 handful of spinach leaves, peel and chop 1 orange, chop 1 dsp of almonds. Mix together with a little yoghourt, sprinkle with dill, dried in winter and fresh in season.

Green Salad

Use all of these, or as available:

lettuce, spinach, cabbage, sprouts, beetroot leaves, watercress, mustard and cress, mint borage, lemon balm

chives or spring onion chickweed (grows wild in most gardens) parsley, comfrey leaves a little onion

Chop or shred and mix together with a little vinegar and oil dressing, yoghourt dressing or orange juice for a change.

Asparagus – the Turkish way

A little costly perhaps, but a real treat!
Cut asparagus into bite size pieces and boil in a little water until soft. Drain, keeping liquid to use in your drinks. While still warm arrange in a dish and pour over yoghourt dressing No. 1 (see p. 109), garnish with chopped dill, chives or both. Tarragon also makes a delicious addition to the sauce.

Avocado Matador

Serves 2

1 avocado	1 small clove garlic
¼ melon in small chunks, or cucumber if allowed	2 medium lettuce leaves
	2 large strawberries
juice of ¼ lemon	1 tsp fresh basil or mint, chopped

Halve the avocado, remove stone and scoop out the flesh carefully, taking care not to break the skin. Place flesh in a dish and mash with melon chunks, lemon juice and crushed garlic. Shred the lettuce finely and mix into the avocado flesh, together with the basil or mint. Spoon the mixture into the avocado skins and dress with thin slices of strawberry.

You can adapt this recipe for other members of the family by adding prawns to the mixture.

Try this variation:

Stuffed Avocado with Alfalfa

Halve an avocado, scoop out flesh and mash with 2 tsp lemon juice. Add alfalfa sprouts, 1 dsp raisins or sultanas. Pile back into shell and serve sprinkled with a little fresh mint.

Peach and Lentil Sprout Salad

2 peaches	½ grapefruit
175g (6oz) lentil sprouts	a little chopped mint

Chop the peaches into thin slices. Add the lentil sprouts. Dress with the juice of ½ a grapefruit and a little chopped mint if desired.

Green Salad with Tofu

½ bunch watercress, chopped	1 small courgette, cut into sticks
½ tray mustard and cress	1 unripe pear, grated
2 lettuce leaves, finely chopped	50g (2oz) tofu cut into small cubes

Mix all together and dress with a vinaigrette dressing containing fresh herbs e.g. marjoram, basil.

Further Suggestions for Salads

It is important not to get used to relying on the usual type of salad such as lettuce, tomato and cucumber, particularly as the two latter foods are listed with a caution in Appendix 1. Be very sparing with oil and garlic.

1. **Carrot and beetroot.** Dressing of lemon juice, a drop of oil, and caraway seed.
2. **Watercress, bean sprouts and corn.** Dressing of cider vinegar, chopped mint and a little honey.
3. **Lettuce, cucumber and tomato.** Dressing of garlic, lemon juice and cider vinegar, sprinkled with chopped fresh mint.
4. **Avocado, lettuce and basil.** Dressing of oil and lemon juice.
5. **Courgette, lettuce and radish.** Dressing of oil and cider vinegar.
6. **Beetroot and cooking apple.** Dressing of lemon juice and oil or cider vinegar and oil.
7. **Mustard and cress and lentil sprouts.**
8. **Sunflower sprouts, grated carrot and chopped mint.** Dressing of lemon juice.
9. **Fennel, celery and wheat sprouts with peas and watercress.**
10. **Sweetcorn Sunshine.** Sweetcorn boiled and scraped off the cob, lettuce strips, cauliflower florets, as they are or sliced, and cress. Dressing of garlic, lemon juice and a spot of oil.

11. **Couscous and orange.** Soak couscous in boiling water for 15–20 minutes, separate with a fork to help to cool and prevent lumps. When cool add chopped watercress, parsley and bean sprouts. Serve with a French dressing.

12. **Courgette and orange.** Courgette, celery, orange and lentil sprouts. Serve with a dressing of avocado, yoghourt and garlic.

13. **Jamaican.** Grated carrot, with desiccated coconut and currants. Toss in lemon juice. Sunflower seeds may also be added for colour and texture.

14. **Alfalfa and banana.** Alfalfa sprouts, cashews, apple and raisins, with a dressing of mashed banana and lemon juice.

SALAD DRESSINGS

Yoghourt Dressing

1) Mix together:
**1 tbs yoghourt
1 onion, finely chopped
a little crushed garlic
1 tsp lemon juice**

2) Liquidise or mix together:
**1 tbs yoghourt
1 clove garlic, crushed
½ tsp tarragon, fresh or if
dried soaked in lemon juice
for 1 hour
½ tsp paprika**

Lemon and Oil Dressing

1 tbs lemon juice

**2 tsp safflower, or sunflower
seed oil (all cold-pressed)**

Avocado Dressing

Blend in a liquidiser:
**½ avocado (flesh of)
juice of ½ lemon**

**1 clove garlic
½ onion, or add chopped
chives after liquidising**

Avocado and Cashew Dressing

Blend in your liquidiser:
100g (4oz) cashew nuts   **150ml (¼ pt) water**
½ avocado (flesh of)   **½ chopped onion**
lemon juice to taste

Sunflower Dressing or Dip

Blend in your liquidiser:
100g (4oz) sunflower seeds   **1 stick celery**
1 clove garlic   **juice of ½ lemon**

Add a little water if you want to use it as dressing. For a change you could use this as a dip with suitable vegetables (i.e. carrots, celery, spring onions, cauliflower florets) around it.

SOUPS

Spinach Soup

Make a roux with 2 tsp oil, 1 dsp wholemeal flour, and add enough water, or vegetable stock if you have any, to make it to soup consistency. Chop spinach leaves and cook in the sauce for approx 3–5 minutes, take off the heat and put through a liquidiser. This can be done with all leaf vegetables, i.e. watercress, lettuce, and also cauliflower, if you chop it into small pieces before cooking. Try adding finely chopped onions, either to the roux or with the vegetables.

Lentil and Onion Soup

75g (3oz) lentils   **1 medium onion, chopped or**
450ml (¾ pt) water   **in rings**
1 tsp oil   **few pieces of celery**
1 carrot   **1 bay leaf, some cloves**
                                    chopped chives or parsley

Wash lentils and cook in the water and oil for approx 10 minutes, then add chopped vegetables and stir these in. Bring to the boil and simmer gently until all is cooked. Add more water if necessary. Add a little lemon juice and serve sprinkled with parsley or chives or both. Liquidise if preferred smooth.

Onion and Carrot Soup

1 large onion	**2 medium carrots**
a little cooked rice if you have any left over	

Chop vegetables and cook in water until tender. Liquidise and add a little milk, if allowed. Serve sprinkled with chopped parsley and brewers' yeast.

Sweet Potato Soup

Lightly sauté 1 onion, add 2 chopped (not peeled) sweet potatoes and gently cook with 300ml (½ pt) (or more if necessary) water until soft. Liquidise with 1 dsp cold-pressed oil and a pinch of nutmeg. Serve with chopped chives.

Pea Soup

Try this uncooked soup, which can be eaten cold in summer or gently warmed in winter.
Liquidise 225g (8oz) fresh garden peas, with 300ml (½ pt) fresh carrot juice and a pinch of nutmeg. Then add the flesh of ½ avocado chopped and a few chopped chives. Sprinkle with Brewers yeast or golden yeast, if liked.

Leek and Potato Soup

2 large leeks, washed and chopped	**1 medium potato with skin, well scrubbed and chopped**
some ground nuts	**into cubes**

Boil in water until soft and liquidise. Add a little lemon juice or cider vinegar to taste and serve sprinkled with brewers' yeast and chopped chives.

Leek and Jerusalem Artichoke Soup

Sauté:

1 leek, chopped	1 bay leaf
2–3 artichokes, chopped	1 clove of garlic
2 carrots, chopped	a little basil

Add 600ml (1 pt) of vegetable stock and cook until soft, liquidise and serve sprinkled with a little dill.

Spiced Vegetable Soup

1 medium onion	1 turnip or swede
2 medium carrots	a little cabbage
1 leek	

Chop and cook in a little water until soft, adding 1 tsp each of aniseed, marjoram and dill. Either liquidise or eat as a 'hot-pot' type of soup sprinkled with brewers' yeast and/or seaweed and parsley.

Creamed Onion Soup

225g (8oz) chopped onion	1 dsp oil
1 tbs wholemeal flour	600ml (1 pt) water or stock

Boil onion in the stock or water until tender. Heat oil in a saucepan and add flour, and stir in the onion and water. Add a little more water, if too thick. Liquidise and serve sprinkled with brewers' yeast and chopped parsley.

Summerfruit Soup

100g (¼lb) strawberries (any other soft fruit can be used, remove stones)	300ml (½ pt) strong vegetable stock

Liquidise and simmer for 1–2 minutes, cool and blend in 1 tbs yoghourt and serve with chopped mint or lemon balm, or chives.

SAUCES, CASSEROLES AND HOT DISHES

Cooked dishes must be eaten after the raw salads.

Baked Sweet Potatoes

These are not related to ordinary potatoes but can be washed and baked in their skins in the same way. Serve with a vegetable casserole, or salad with yoghourt dressing.

Baked Vegetable Casserole with Tahini and Coriander Sauce

1 medium onion, chopped	1 carrot, chopped
1 leek	some artichokes (Jerusalem)

Put in a casserole with a little water and bake in the oven until tender. Make a white sauce with wholemeal flour and oil, add liquid from the casserole, a little lemon juice, 1 level tbs tahini and ½ tsp coriander (more if liked). Pour over casserole and serve hot.

Vegetable Casserole (1)

1 medium carrot, chopped	1 onion, chopped
a little celery, chopped	1 tsp each of sage and thyme
2 dsp brown lentils	½ cooking apple, chopped
1 dsp oatflakes for thickening	

Cover with water or stock and bake in the oven in a tight fitting casserole until tender.

Vegetable Casserole (2)

Serves 2

In this variation, fennel adds a subtle flavour.

enough ghee to sauté
1 onion, peeled and sliced
2 medium carrots, scrubbed and sliced
1 stick celery, washed and sliced
2–3 slices fresh fennel, washed
1 clove garlic, peeled and sliced
1 medium potato, washed and sliced (do not peel unless old potato)
4 broad beans (young ones), washed and sliced with pods
6 pods shelled peas
2 large florets cauliflower, washed
1 bay leaf
½ tsp mixed herbs
½ tsp dried mint
vegetable stock

Heat ghee gently in a saucepan and sauté onion, carrot, celery, fennel and garlic for about 3 minutes. Place all vegetables and herbs in a pot and cover with vegetable stock. Cook in the oven until the vegetables are just done.

Adaptation for the family: Any left-overs of meat may be added once your portion has been removed, or you could sauté the left-over meat in a little ghee, add a little sage and serve with the stew. All left-over meat should be kept covered in a refrigerator for not more than a couple of days.

Roast Vegetable Casserole

Scrub well and chop the following vegetables:
Sweet potato, leek, carrot, artichoke, onion (peeled)
Parboil and place all in a ready-oiled oven dish. Sauté some garlic in a little oil and pour over the vegetables. Roast in the oven until tender. Serve with lentil sauce.

Lentil Sauce

Cook a quantity of green lentils with some carrots, onions, turnips and garlic. When soft purée in liquidiser, adding dill, basil and sage (or mint). (If necessary thicken this with wholemeal flour.)

Vegetable Bake

Serves 2

2 onions, peeled and sliced in rings	1 tbs chopped mint
2 carrots, washed and sliced in rings	1½ tbs oil
2 large potatoes (sweet potatoes can be used), washed and sliced	1 small clove garlic, peeled and crushed
	1 tbs sesame seeds

Steam onions, carrots and potatoes until just cooked.
Place in an oiled ovenproof dish in layers, putting the mint in between each layer.
Mix the garlic in the oil, brush over the potatoes and sprinkle with sesame seeds. Bake in a fairly hot oven until the potatoes turn golden-brown and are slightly crisp.

Winter Borscht

1 dsp oil	1 onion
1 large beetroot, grated	1 carrot, grated
450g (1lb) red cabbage, chopped	

Lightly sauté all vegetables in the oil and then add water to cover. Simmer until vegetables are tender, add ½ cup tomato juice, chopped fresh (or dried) dill and parsley. Serve sprinkled with brewers' yeast and a spoonful of yoghourt.

Spinach Catalan

Serves 2

450g (1lb) spinach   50g (2oz) sultanas or raisins
50g (2oz) toasted pinekernels

Wash spinach in several waters and drain. Cook in a tightly
lidded pan with only 2 tbs water for 7 minutes. Chop roughly.
Serve onto a warmed plate and spread out into a round. Scatter
on raisins or sultanas. Toast pinekernels and sprinkle on top.
(Makes a very substantial vegetable course or main dish.)

Stuffed Marrow (1)

Serves 4

100g (4oz) beans (soaked   100g (4oz) wholewheat
overnight)   breadcrumbs (soft)
2 medium onions, or more   50g (2oz) chopped brazil
cold-pressed sunflower oil   nuts
1 medium marrow   25g (1oz) sultanas
                                  1 tsp savory, or other herb

Simmer beans until very soft, large ones about 1 hour, small
ones about ½ hour. Sauté chopped onion in oil. Cut marrow in
half lengthways and peel if skin is hard. Scoop out seeds.
Simmer marrow very gently until partly cooked, 5–10 minutes.

Heat a little oil in an ovenproof dish. Mix mashed beans,
crumbs, nuts, onions, sultanas and herbs and pile into marrow
boats. Sprinkle with a little of the hot oil and bake at 190°C
(375°F), gas mark 5 for about 40 minutes. Serve sprinkled with
chopped parsley.

Stuffed Marrow (2)

Serves 2

A good way of using up any left-over rice.

1 small thick marrow, approx. 675–900g (1½–2lb)	1 tsp parsley, washed and chopped
50g (2oz) ghee	1 dsp sage
1 small onion	3 dsp left-over savoury rice (see p. 125)
1 large mushroom (or 2 small), washed and chopped	freshly grated nutmeg
1 dsp sultanas, washed	some chopped nuts
1 clove garlic, crushed	

Wash marrow and cut into 5cm thick rings. There is no need to remove the skin if the marrow is young and tender. Remove seeds and place rings in a lidded pan with a little water, or steam, until beginning to soften. Remove and place in an oven dish in single layers.

Gently heat the ghee and sauté the onion. Add the mushroom, sultanas, garlic, parsley, sage and the cooked rice. Fill the rings with the mixture and sprinkle with nutmeg. Dot with ghee if there is any over.

Place in a moderate oven, 190°C (375°F), gas mark 5, until cooked to your taste. To serve, sprinkle with chopped nuts and a bit of parsley to decorate, if permitted.

Adaptation for the family: Any left-overs of minced meat can be added to the mixture.

Stuffed Courgettes

Halve courgettes, scoop out centre and fill with:

1 onion, peeled and chopped	2–3 tbs breadcrumbs
2 mushrooms, chopped (optional)	1 tbs milled almonds
1 clove garlic, crushed	a little thyme

Mix all together and fill courgettes. Place in an ovenproof dish with a little water and bake until tender.

Saucy Cauliflower

Serves 2

1 small cauliflower, washed
and trimmed
½ tsp paprika
1 tsp chopped parsley

1 tbs chopped nuts
Roux: Equal parts ghee or oil
and wholewheat flour
soya milk

Place the cauliflower in boiling water and cook until just tender. To make the roux sauce, place equal quantities of oil or ghee and flour in a pan and heat, stirring continuously with a wooden spoon, for 2–3 minutes. It will resemble a near solid mass. Add the soya milk a little at a time. Beat vigorously until the mixture leaves the sides of the pan clean. If lumps appear, use a whisk to help break down the consistency. Allow the mixture to thicken between each addition of liquid until you have a sauce that is the consistency you require. Simmer for about 5 minutes, stirring occasionally to avoid sticking. Remove from the heat.

Place cauliflower in a heatproof dish and pour over the sauce. Just before serving sprinkle on paprika, parsley and chopped nuts.

Adaptation for the family: If you wish, grated cheese can be added to the sauce after your own portion is removed. Season with whatever you fancy.

Sweetcorn Chowder

Serves 4

2 ears of sweetcorn, cooked
and corn cut off the cob
600ml (1 pt) hot water
100g (4oz) cashews

2 spring onions
½ tsp celery seeds
1 tbs oil/ghee

Blend all together in a liquidiser and heat through. Garnish with sprouted seeds or parsley. Try using spinach, watercress or celery instead of sweetcorn.

Chinese Vegetables

Suggested vegetables: bean sprouts, celery, carrots, courgettes, peas, cauliflower, broad beans, tofu. Cook in steamer until just tender, then toss in toasted sesame seeds. Serve with ginger and cashew sauce.

Ginger and Cashew Sauce

2 tsp grated ginger	100g (4oz) cashews
225g (½lb) onions	450ml (¾ pt) stock
2 cloves garlic	3 tsp arrowroot
ghee to sauté	

Sauté the ginger, onion and garlic in ghee for 5 minutes. Then mix with other ingredients and liquidise in the blender. Heat through until thickened slightly. Garnish with parsley.

Stuffed Mushrooms

Serves 4–6

1 cup cooked brown rice	1 tsp coriander
1 cup breadcrumbs	1 tsp tarragon
parsley, chopped finely	1 tbs ghee
100g (4oz) tofu	about 12 large mushrooms
2 cloves garlic, chopped finely	

Mix all ingredients together, and pile the stuffing in the hollow of the mushrooms. Bake for about 10 minutes in a hot oven, 220°C (425°F), gas mark 7. Also try this stuffing in baked onions.

Savory or dill when cooked with tofu helps to eliminate gas in the stomach.

Bulgar Surprise

Serves 4–6

100g (4oz) dried apricots	450g (1lb) broad beans
100g (4oz) onions, chopped	4 bay leaves
4 cloves garlic, chopped finely	fresh basil
ghee to sauté	fresh mint
350g (12oz) bulgar wheat	1 tsp nutmeg
3 courgettes	
3 carrots	

Cook the apricots until soft then liquidise. Sauté the onions and garlic in ghee for 5 minutes. Add bulgar and cook for 3 minutes, stirring. Add boiling water. Cook for 10 minutes, then take off heat. Steam all the remaining vegetables with the herbs. Serve the vegetables on a bed of bulgar wheat and cover with apricot sauce.

Legumes, Pulses and Nuts

To give you the right amount of protein when you do not eat meat, there are the pulses, and of course nuts and seeds, and yoghourt. It is important that you have as much variety of 'protein foods' as possible so that your diet is properly balanced.

Lentil Dish

Serves 3–4

225g (8oz) brown lentils	50g (2oz) sultanas
225g (½lb) carrots	a few cloves
1 medium onion	bay leaf

Soak lentils, well covered with water, for 20 minutes. Slice carrots and peel, but do not slice, onion. Put these and the rest of the ingredients in with the lentils and bring to the boil. Simmer for ½ hour, remove onion, slice and sauté, put back and mix. Check at intervals that the water does not dry up. A little liquid should remain at the end of cooking time.

Mixed Bean Stew

1 dsp butter beans	2 dsp wholewheat
1 dsp haricot or adzuki beans	1 dsp mung beans

Soak overnight in water, discard the water, cover with fresh water and then cook until soft. The mung beans do not take very long to cook (20 minutes) so add them a little later to prevent them going soft and mushy. To give flavour add onion, bay leaves, garlic, and a little ginger. Serve hot, dressed with a little oil, sprinkled with brewers' yeast and chopped fresh parsley and rosemary, or cold as part of a salad.

Bean and Grain Casserole

Use any kind of dried beans and/or peas, or lentils and any kind of whole grain (i.e. brown rice, pot-barley, rye, buckwheat, millet, wheat) and soak overnight.

2 large onions, chopped	vegetable stock or water
oil to sauté	100g (4oz) apricots (if liked)
100g (4oz) grain	garlic (if liked)
100g (4oz) beans	plenty of herbs (dill, basil, oregano, or bay)

Sauté onions in oil in two saucepans, add soaked cereal to one pan, beans to the other, and cover with hot stock or water. Cover with close-fitting lids and simmer on top of stove or in oven. Water should mostly be absorbed. Towards the end of cooking time add apricots, garlic and a generous amount of herbs.

Nut Roast

100g (4oz) brazil nuts	100g (4oz) fresh breadcrumbs
100g (4oz) onion	100g (4oz) carrots
3 level tbs soya flour mixed with sage or rosemary to taste	a little oil
	water to cream

Sauté finely chopped onion and carrot, mill nuts, crumbs, sage, or any other favourite herb. Mix all together and spread in a tin, sprinkled with sesame seeds and a little oil. Bake at 180°C (350°F) gas mark 4, for 30–40 minutes.

Lentil Burgers

Serves 2

1 cup cooked lentil purée
½ cup raw chopped nuts (almonds, walnuts or pecans)
1 dsp ground sunflower seeds
1 small chopped onion, sautéd

1 dsp breadcrumbs (wholemeal), or raw oatmeal
sprinkling of sage
sprinkling of celery seeds
1½ tbs oil

Mix all the ingredients together, form into burgers, brush with oil and bake until golden-brown.

An alternative method, equally simple and delicious is:

Almond and Lentil Burgers

Serves 4–6

225g (8oz) red lentils
2 or 3 bay leaves
100g (4oz) ground sunflower seeds

100g (4oz) ground almonds
1 clove garlic, chopped finely (optional)

Boil the lentils with the bay leaves until they are soft, making sure not to use too much water or the burgers will be too mushy. Mix with the other ingredients and form into shape. Brush with a little oil and bake at 200°C (400°F), gas mark 6 for 40 minutes or until browned. Serve with your favourite gravy or sauce.

Soya Surprise

Serves 4

¼ pack arame seaweed	225g (½lb) carrots
225g (½lb) onions	225g (½lb) courgettes
2 cloves garlic, chopped finely	225g (½lb) soya beans, cooked
ghee to sauté	sage to season

Soak seaweed in water. Sauté onions and garlic in a little ghee. Add carrots, courgettes, soya beans and drained seaweed. Cook for 2–3 minutes. Add a little of the water in which the seaweed was soaked, and sage. Cover with a tight lid and cook until the vegetables are tender (about 10 minutes).

Nutty Balls

Makes about 15 balls

1 onion, chopped finely	175g (6oz) lentils, boiled with 3 bay leaves
1 clove garlic, chopped finely	100g (4oz) breadcrumbs
ghee to sauté	1 carrot, grated
225g (8oz) brazil nuts, ground	1 stick celery, grated

Sauté onion and garlic in a little ghee. Mix with all other ingredients and form into balls about the size of a golf ball and place in an oiled baking tray. Cover with Sauce Espagnole (see below) and bake in a hot oven, 200°C (400°F), gas mark 6, for 45 minutes.

Sauce Espagnole

3 spring onions	wholewheat flour to thicken
1 stick celery	vegetable stock
1 carrot	juice of 1 lemon
1 clove garlic	a little tofu (crumbled)
ghee to sauté	basil and mint (fresh if possible)

Cut the vegetables into small pieces and sauté in ghee. Add wholewheat flour to make a roux. Cook over gentle heat for

1–2 minutes. Add vegetable stock, lemon juice, tofu and herbs and heat until thickened.

Millet Patties

Serves 2

2 cups of millet, cooked (steam if possible)
¼ cup of ground peanuts or cashews, or any other nuts you like
2 tsp oil

small chopped onion
sprinkle of celery seeds (not too many), rosemary and thyme for flavour

Mix all ingredients and form into patties. Bake in the oven until golden-brown. You may wish to brush with a little oil to aid browning. This dish is high in protein.

RICE

Always use brown rice, which has a much nicer flavour than white. It is also much better food value because it still has the outer skin which contains a useful amount of vitamin B, iron and calcium, which the white rice lacks. Brown rice takes a little longer than white to cook and it has a more nutty flavour.

Hints on cooking rice: If the rice is stirred too vigorously when placed in the pan the outer coating will break and you will have a rather gluey consistency instead of a fluffy texture. If the lid of the pan is kept on the rice will not burn.

It is a good idea to cook more than is needed to use for other recipes the next day, but it is necessary for rice that is left over to be cooled and placed in a refrigerator; if left in a warm place it can cause sickness and diarrhoea.

Savoury Rice

Serves 2

Enough ghee just to prevent the pan from catching	Vegetable stock or water (1 part rice/2 parts liquid)
1 large carrot, washed and sliced (do not peel)	1 tsp fresh or dried basil, chopped
1 small onion, peeled and chopped	1 tsp fresh or dried mint, chopped
100g (4oz) long grain brown rice, washed	1 large bay leaf

Garnish: chopped chives, sunflower seeds or sesame seeds

Heat ghee gently in a pan and sauté the carrot and onion pieces. Add rice and gently mix with a wooden spoon. Bring the stock or water to the boil and add to the rice with the herbs. Cover the pan and simmer for approximately 30 minutes until the rice is cooked. Remove the bay leaf and serve the rice in a warm dish, garnished with the chives and/or seeds.

A variation is:

Savoury Rice with Mushrooms

100g (4oz) brown rice	1 tsp oil
1 cup boiling water	1 tsp mixed herbs or sage (fresh)
1 large onion	
50g (2oz) mushrooms	1 tbs chopped cucumber

Wash rice, bring the water to the boil, add the oil, rice, and chopped vegetables. Bring back to the boil, and then simmer gently with lid closed for 30 minutes. Add sunflower seeds, raisins and dill seeds.

Rice El Greco

Serves 2

This is a cheap, sustaining dish made from any left-over savoury rice.

8 fresh vine leaves or cabbage leaves	**½ lemon**
savoury rice left-overs	**vegetable stock or water**
freshly chopped mint	

Blanch cabbage leaves or vine leaves until they are pliable enough to fold. Remove any coarse stalks. Spread out the leaves, spoon on the rice mixture and sprinkle liberally with the mint. Fold into neat parcels and pack either in layers or singly side-by-side into a lidded pan. Squeeze over lemon juice and pour over enough vegetable stock or water to cover. Place a plate over the leaves to prevent them from floating and breaking up during cooking, and cover with the pan lid. Simmer until the leaves are cooked, about 45 minutes.

To adapt the recipe for the family, any left-over minced meat can be added to the rice, plus seasoning if required.

Rice Salad

Boil 100g (4oz) rice in 1 cup of water, with a bay leaf and a little rosemary. When cooked, cool and dress with a little oil and cider vinegar. Add chopped fresh parsley and chives or raw chopped onion and apricots (soaked and chopped).

Rice with Herbs

Instead of cooking the rice as above, with all the herbs, try boiling it with the bay leaf, but adding fresh chopped rosemary, sage, chives, lemon balm and parsley after cooking when it has cooled. Dress with a little cider vinegar and oil and garlic dressing.

Rice Pilaff

100g (4oz) rice	1 medium onion, chopped
1 stick celery	50g (2oz) sultanas or
1 leek	chopped apricots

Boil in water (1–1¼ cups) until tender. Serve dressed with 1 tsp oil, sprinkled with chopped almonds (whole, not skinned) and a little banana, if liked.

Rice, Cashew and Broccoli Risotto

Serves 2

75g (3oz) brown rice	half a medium size
1 small onion	broccoli
1 clove garlic	1 corn on the cob
1 tbs ghee	50g (2oz) cashews
a little rosemary and	ground nutmeg and cloves to
tarragon	season
100g (4oz) spinach	parsley, chopped

Boil the rice. Finely chop the onion and garlic and sauté in the ghee for 5 minutes with the rosemary and tarragon. Steam the spinach, broccoli and corn until tender (this can be done in a sieve over the rice). Toast the cashews under the grill. Mix all together and add a little ground nutmeg and cloves to season. Garnish with chopped parsley.

DESSERTS

Apricot Fool

Serves 4–6

225g (½lb) dried apricots	175g (6oz) tofu
apple juice	½ vanilla pod

Soak apricots for 2 hours. Liquidise in blender with apple juice (to required consistency), tofu and vanilla.

Fool with Raspberries and Almonds

Serves 4

2 peaches	100g (4oz) tofu
2 bananas	½ vanilla pod

Liquidise in blender and top with unsulphured flaked almonds and raspberries.

Fruit and Yoghourt Fool

For this you can use any variety of fresh fruit, grate it or mash it and add 2 tbs yoghourt and mix well. It is easiest to do it in a liquidiser. Serve sprinkled with chopped almonds, walnuts, brazil nuts or sesame seeds. Suggested fruit: soaked apricots, or fresh ones, raspberries, blackberries, apples, bananas, oranges or peaches.

Orange and Banana Surprise

Liquidise 1 orange, 1 banana with a little lemon juice and serve sprinkled with a few sultanas and sesame seeds.

Apple and Grapefruit Cocktail

Chop 1 medium apple. Peel ½ grapefruit and chop. Mix together and serve with a few grapes on top.

Apple and Wheatgerm Surprise

Grate 1 medium apple and toss in a little lemon or orange juice; put in a dish. Mix together:

½ tsp chopped rosemary (fresh)	1 tsp wheatgerm
1 tsp sunflower seeds	

Sprinkle this over the top of the apple.

Baked Apple

Cut out centre of 1 large dessert apple and fill with:

½ tbs ground brazil nuts	½ tsp ground coriander
½ tbs ground cinnamon	1 tbs sultanas or currants

Bake in the oven until soft at 180°C (350°F) gas mark 4.

Apple Mousse

Finely grate or liquidise 2 dessert apples, add a little lemon juice and a little ginger and cinnamon. Serve sprinkled with sesame seeds or almonds (chopped).

Nut Creams

These can be used as you would real cream. They are delicious with fresh fruits or you could make these into savoury sandwich spreads or dips by adding fresh chopped herbs, onion or garlic, etc.

150g (5oz) almonds or cashew nuts	**150ml (5 fl.oz) water**

Liquidise until creamy.

By adding a little lemon juice, real vanilla from a pod, a little more water depending on the consistency and different fruits i.e. banana, apple, peaches, apricots, you will have a whole range of desserts. Nut Creams are very rich, and should therefore be kept as a treat or special occasion, certainly not as an everyday food.

Calypso Cream

For a dessert with a tropical flavour try: bananas, apples, peaches, creamed coconut and cinnamon, liquidised together and topped with soft fruit such as cherries or raspberries.

Fruit Bliss

Cut in half and stone either a nectarine or peach. Grind some cashews, mix with coconut and a little honey, fill the cavity of the fruit and brown slightly under the grill. You may like to just sprinkle ground almonds on the fruit and eat.

Fruit Purée with Crunchy Topping

50g (2oz) soaked dried apricots	**1 banana**
50g (2oz) sunflower seeds (dried or sprouted)	**juice of ½ a lemon**
1 orange	**1 apple**

Blend together in a liquidiser.

Topping

100g (4oz) muesli base (see p. 102)	**50g (2oz) sunflower seeds**
50g (2oz) sultanas or raisins	**50g (2oz) coconut**
50g (2oz) flaked almonds	

Mix together and toast under the grill until golden. Sprinkle thickly over fruit purée. This topping will keep for some time in an airtight tin.

Banana Cream Pie

Serves 6–8

Pastry

approx. ⅔ cup sunflower oil/ghee	**450g (1lb) wholewheat flour**
⅓ cup water	**100g (4oz) soya flour**

Mix oil and water. Add to flour and stir lightly until the dough rounds up into a ball. This pastry may be a little crumbly so it is a good idea to roll it out between greaseproof paper. Line a flan tin with the pastry and cover the bottom with dried beans to keep level. Bake at 200°C (400°F), gas mark 6, for about 20 minutes, removing beans a few minutes before end of cooking time. This pastry can also be used for savoury dishes.

Filling

100g (4oz) dates	2 tbs arrowroot
225g (8oz) cashews	1 vanilla pod (optional)
1 tsp grated orange rind	2 large bananas
2 cups water	

Blend all ingredients except bananas in liquidiser until smooth. Heat in a saucepan until mixture thickens. Leave to cool.

Meanwhile, slice bananas into the baked pie shell. Pour the cooled mixture over this and refrigerate to set further. Garnish with coconut before serving.

Fruit Salads

A few tips for preparation:
1. Some fruits such as apples and bananas go brown when cut, so eat straight away or toss in a little lemon juice.
2. Add to the natural juice of the fruit – try apple juice, a little wine or a sauce made from cooked hunza apricots.
3. Add a little dried fruit, nuts, coconut or sesame seeds. Sprouted sunflower seeds or sprouted wheat are particularly good – they have a natural sweetness.

When you are fed up with fruit salad, make yourself a nice happy face to cheer yourself up. Cut a thin slice through a watermelon and put it on a plate. On top of this put grapes for the eyes, half a pear for the nose and half a banana for the mouth. Sprinkle coconut or sunflower seeds for the eyebrows and hair.

Exotic Fruit

With local shops and supermarkets now bringing exotic fruits into our reach, it would be good to let friends or relatives know that, if they wish to buy you a gift, fruit would be received with as much pleasure as flowers. The following are just a few examples:

Cape gooseberries. The fruit of the plant *Physalis peruviana*, these small orange berries are encased in papery 'Chinese lanterns'. They can be eaten fresh, stewed or made into preserves. They will keep well if bought unripe.

Chinese gooseberries (kiwi fruit). About the size of a large plum, they have a brown hairy skin (which you peel and discard) and green flesh, beautifully patterned in the centre with dark seeds. The fruit is sweet and juicy and the taste is a cross between a strawberry and a gooseberry.

Lychees or litchis. Chinese in origin, these round fruits have a hard, scaly skin turning through pink to brown. Buy when the skins are red and avoid any shrivelled ones. The white, pulpy flesh is firm and slippery with a perfumed flavour.

Mangoes. They come in various sizes and shapes and their tough skins can be green, yellow, orange or red with a blush of pink. The juicy flesh is orange-yellow when ripe and has a delicate fragrance and spicy flavour.

Papayas (sometimes known as pawpaws). Similar in shape to a large plum, these fruits have smooth, green to yellow and orange skins, juicy, orange-pink pulp which is melon-like in texture, and large black seeds.

Passion fruit. The size of a large plum, this fruit has a purple, wrinkled skin when ripe. The orange-coloured pulp is sweet, juicy and aromatic in flavour.

Persimmons. Looking like large tomatoes, persimmons have leathery skins which turn from yellow to bright red. Eat when red, juicy and soft. If you do not particularly like the sharp flavour, try mixing this fruit in the blender with another fruit.

Pomegranates. These are the size of large oranges, with thin, tough skin. When ripe the fruit is pink or bright red and the juice crimson. The pulp is packed with seeds which are sucked for the flesh and then discarded as they have a slightly bitter taste.

Home Made Yoghourt

This is very simple and easy to make, provided you follow a few basic rules. Firstly, always bring the milk to the boil, then allow it to cool to around 37°C (99°F). This destroys the growth factor *all* milks contain that encourages cancer to grow. Milk is baby food not adult food. Make sure your vessels are kept scrupulously clean as the yoghourt bacteria are very delicate and easily spoiled. Place a little bought yoghourt in the bottom of a container and add the cooled milk, whisk well, and leave for approx 5–7 hours in a warm place. It should then be thick. Keep in fridge and use as required.

The easiest and most reliable method is probably to buy one of the inexpensive yoghourt makers, like the Bel, and follow their instructions. Always buy live yoghourt culture as your starter: any health food shop sells it. However, if you wash containers thoroughly to remove all traces of old yoghourt, boil them and keep one small container closed to use as a starter for the next lot, you need not use a fresh bought starter each time.

Use fresh goat's milk to make your yoghourt wherever possible. Goat's milk is less acid, and much easier to digest.

DRINKS AND JUICES

Fresh Fruit and Vegetable Juices

Pure and undiluted grape juice can be bought from any health food shop and kept in the fridge. Orange or grapefruit (or indeed any fruit juice) is best freshly pressed. When it comes to vegetable juices this becomes very difficult and you really need an electric juicer. You just scrub well and chop the vegetables of your choice and put them into the juicer, turn on and wait for it to do the work!

A juicer is essential for you to make the 4–6 glasses of fresh carrot juice that you should be taking every day. This amount will take about 3kg (7lb) of carrots. To make the necessary vitamin A and carotene available to do their work, the juice must be emulsified with a teaspoon of cold-pressed oil and thoroughly whisked to distribute it evenly. Drink it as soon as it is made.

Remember that all drinks are to be taken ½ hour before meals.

Carrot Juice

Because carrot juice plays a large part in your health programme, you may find that adding other ingredients to the juice helps you to enjoy the drink a bit more.
Try the following variations:
Put fresh mint in the juicer or add, chopped, afterwards.
Add beetroot juice, mint and lemon juice (a good blood tonic drink).
Add apple and basil.
Liquidise alfalfa sprouts and mix in with the juice. This is a very good way of taking large quantities of these valuable sprouts.
Add celery, parsley, spinach and watercress to the liquidiser. This drink is high in potassium but remember that celery and parsley are not to be taken often by cancer patients.
Add alfalfa, parsley, spinach and watercress. Also high in potassium and an excellent tonic.

Mulled Apple Juice

Heat gently in a pan:

300ml (½ pt) fresh apple juice	1 tsp honey
2–3 cloves	a little cinnamon
small piece lemon peel	

Strain and drink hot, or in the warm weather cold, with ice.

Orange Drink

Blend in your liquidiser:

300ml (½ pt) fresh orange juice	Slice of fresh pineapple
2 sprigs fresh mint	
or 150ml (¼ pt) mint tea	

This is also very nice with apple juice. Perhaps it will give you ideas for other combinations.

Cashew and Orange Drink

Liquidise 2 cups of orange juice, 2 tbs coconut and a handful of cashews.

Banana Milk Shake

200ml (⅓ pt) water (or apple juice)	**3 or 4 dates**
	¼ vanilla pod
1 ripe banana	**1 tsp sunflower oil**
50g (2oz) cashews	

Blend all ingredients in a liquidiser until creamy and smooth. Makes one tall glass.

Cashew Cream

Similar to banana milk shake but thicker. Good instead of cream on desserts.

300ml (½ pt) water	**1 tsp oil**
100g (4oz) cashews	**(a little honey if needed)**
½ vanilla pod	

Liquidise all ingredients in a blender. This can be flavoured with fruit if you wish (or sugarless fruit juice concentrate).

Soya Milk

Soak 225g (½lb) soya beans for two days, changing water twice a day. Liquidise the soaked beans with 1.5 litres (2½ pts) water. Strain well through muslin. Heat liquid in a saucepan until almost boiling and then strain again. Place in a blender adding a chopped vanilla pod and 1 tbs oil. Will keep in the refrigerator.

Herb Teas and Drinks

You will find a good selection of herb teas available in any health food shop. Or you can make your own from fresh herbs grown in the garden. Try putting five or six sage leaves in the teapot, add boiling water and leave to infuse for 5 minutes. As you pour it out add a little lemon juice. Parsley, mint and rosemary can also be prepared like this.

SNACK MEALS AND SPREADS

Do not eat between meals, the stomach must rest in order to work efficiently during the digestion periods. If you feel the urge to eat, just drink a glass of water and wait; this will not only help your body, but satisfy the hunger for a while.

The following recipes are suggestions for light meals at tea time or supper. Always eat the raw foods first, but if you are one of the 'hungry ones' you can fill the gap with couscous and sultanas, and soya milk, or any other bulk food. The spreads are delicious in sandwiches or as dips with raw vegetables. For a quick satisfying meal you could eat salad or fruit with a slice of brown, wholemeal bread.

Hot Tutti Frutti

Serves 2

Soak overnight in 150ml (¼ pt) apple juice the following dried fruits: prunes, apricots, apples, sultanas, figs and some wild apricots (if obtainable – you will need to remove the stones). Simmer in a saucepan for 10–15 minutes the next day. Serve either hot, cold or warm with a topping of tofu cream and chopped nuts.

Adaptation for the family: Pour over some calvados or brandy and serve with cream.

Tofu Cream

Liquidise some tofu and cashews, adding some soya milk if necessary.

Molasses Cookies

equal quantities of: oil,
molasses, rolled oats
double quantity of
wholewheat pastry flour
(finer ground)

vanilla to taste

Mix oil and molasses and thoroughly blend in the rest of the ingredients. Either drop in spoonfuls or spread out on a baking tray and bake for about 15–20 minutes at 170°C (325°F), gas mark 3, until golden brown.

Yeast Biscuits

1 tbs dry active yeast
1 tbs honey

2½ cups wholewheat flour
5 tbs oil

Dissolve the yeast and honey in ½ cup of water and allow to set. Sift the flour and mix in the oil and ½ cup of warm water. Add the yeast mixture and blend lightly. Roll out to approx 2cm thick, cut into shapes as desired, and leave to rise for 20 minutes on a greased, floured tray. Bake for 25–30 minutes at 200°C (400°F), gas mark 6.

Peach and Banana Milk Shake

You may like to take a light meal in liquid form. If so, try the following.

Liquidise ½ peach, ½ banana, some sunflower and sesame seeds, and enough soya milk to make a milk shake consistency. Add a little lemon juice to prevent discolouring. For variety add cashew nuts or prepare with any other fresh fruits in season.

Teatime Suggestions

Avocado and honey sandwiches (go easy on the honey).
Salad sandwiches with sprouts.
Banana pops: Peel a banana and cut into bite-sized pieces. Roll in a little honey and sprinkle with sesame seeds.

Adzuki Bean and Apple Spread

Chop and cook 2 apples, 1 onion, 2 cloves of garlic with ½ tsp of cloves in a little ghee, until a pulp. Liquidise with 225g (8oz) cooked adzuki beans. Makes enough for 4–6.

Banana and Tahini Spread

Mash up 1 banana with 1 tbs of tahini. Put into the blender, adding lemon juice to taste and 1 tsp of sunflower seed oil. Blend until smooth, and use as a spread on wholemeal toast or bread. For variety try adding a few chopped almonds or a few teaspoons of buckwheat, to give this spread a nice, crunchy taste.

Apple and Almond Spread

Chop 1 apple and put into a liquidiser with a few almonds and raisins. Blend until smooth, add a little tahini to bind and 1 tsp oil (safflower) and lemon juice to taste.

Sunflower Seed and Garlic Spread

Liquidise 100g (4oz) sunflower seeds, 1 carrot or apple or both, 1 clove of garlic, a little parsley or sage, and 1 tsp Brewers yeast or golden yeast, if liked. Add some water if too dry.

Apple and Apricot Spread

Liquidise 1 apple with 4 fresh (or dried and then soaked) apricots and 1 tsp cold-pressed oil. You can add a little slippery elm powder to this if you like it thicker, or if you find it difficult to take any other way.

Nut, Seed and Honey Spread

Grind peanuts and sunflower seeds with a little oil and enough honey to make a nice spread.

Fruit and Nut Spread

Liquidise sultanas, dates, figs, or combinations of other dried fruits and almonds with enough orange juice to make a paste.

Apricot Spread

Soak a few dried apricots until soft and liquidise with an equal amount of dates, adding the water from the apricots to make the right consistency.

Avocado Spread

This is very good on wholewheat bread or toast or as a dip for raw vegetables. Mash a ripe avocado and add a little lemon juice, some yoghourt, spring onions or garlic.

Also, try this variation with herbs:

Avocado and Herb Spread

Mash ½ an avocado with a little lemon juice and add any freshly sprouted seeds, and freshly chopped (or dried) herbs such as mint, basil, parsley, comfrey or sage.

Brown Lentil Paté with Apple

Chop and cook 225g (½lb) apples and 1 onion in ghee, until a pulp. Mix with 225g (8oz) boiled Chinese lentils, 1 dsp tahini and 3 bay leaves. Chill before serving. Makes enough for 4–6.

Brown Lentil Paté with Mushrooms

Make in the same way as brown lentil paté with apple but substitute mushrooms for apples. Add lemon juice, parsley and thyme as seasoning.

Butterbean and Parsley Paté

Purée cooked butterbeans with parsley, garlic, lemon juice and coriander.

Humus

Soak overnight 225g (8oz) chick peas, then cook in the same water until tender. Liquidise and add: 2 cloves crushed garlic (or more); 2–3 tbs tahini and 4 tbs oil. Liquidise again and serve with salads (in small quantities) or as a sandwich spread.

SPROUTING GRAINS

Sprouted seeds are highly nutritious. They are rich in vitamins and minerals and contain high quality protein. Sprouting increases the vitamin content of seeds from 4–10 times. Many sprouts may be eaten raw because during the sprouting the starch is changed to simple sugar. They are also really delicious. Methods of sprouting vary slightly according to the seeds or beans used, but in principle it is very easy to do: all you need is a big coffee jar and a piece of muslin to go over the top, secured with an elastic band. Wash the seeds, put them into the jar, and cover the top with muslin. Leave your jar somewhere warm, near the sink preferably, as the seeds have to be rinsed at regular intervals (3 times a day) with cool or tepid water. You fill the jar through the muslin and tip it out. After about 4 days (although beans take a little longer), they are ready to be added to your salads. Some seeds do better if first soaked overnight in warm water.

Theoretically there is nothing that cannot be sprouted as long as it is a seed or bean. Alfalfa seems to be the favourite, since it takes less time than most other seeds. You will also be familiar with mung bean sprouts which have become popular via the Chinese type of cooking. Lentils are delicious sprouted, as are sesame and sunflower seeds, wheat, rye . . . the list is endless.

	Sprouting time	**Best length**
Dry lentils	3 days	12–25mm
Whole sunflower	2–3 days	6mm
Whole mung beans	3–4 days	50–75mm
*Alfalfa	2–3 days	25–50mm
Soya beans	3 days	12–20mm
Whole wheat	2–3 days	6–12mm

* When alfalfa sprouts have reached the required length leave them in the sun to develop a bright green colour.

GHEE

Use unsalted butter and a pan with a lip, made either of stainless steel or good quality enamel.

Melt the butter on a moderate heat and bring it to the boil. With a large spoon, skim off the froth. This process may have to be repeated several times to ensure that all the white deposit is removed from the surface. Continue to boil, reducing the heat. Light coloured flakes of protein will form. When these start to brown, gently pour off the liquid left in the pan, taking care to leave the sediment behind.

This process enables one to eliminate the allergenic proteins and leaves a stable non-carcinogenic cooking fat that retains the delightful flavour of butter. Use it sparingly in cooking. Pour it into small ramekins and cover with clingfilm. It will keep in the refrigerator for some time.

WHOLEMEAL BREAD

You can buy this in health food shops, but it is much better to make your own. A very quick and successful method is the 'Grant Loaf' which is made in no more than an hour. You will find that the delicious smell coming from the oven will make it all worthwhile.

50g (2oz) fresh yeast　　　**2 tsp brown sugar or honey**
750ml (1¼ pt) warm water　**1.3kg (3lb) wholewheat flour**
(more if necessary)　　　　**(100%)**

Cream yeast with the honey or sugar and add a little warm water. Leave it until it starts to bubble, then stir it into the flour with the remaining warm water and knead until all the water is taken up (about 5 minutes). Leave to rise in a warm place for ¼ hour. Divide into four greased baking tins. Put into oven and turn on to approx 150°C (275–300°F), gas mark 2, until the bread has risen over the top of the tins. Then turn up the oven to 200°C (400°F), gas mark 6, and bake for 30–35 minutes. When the bread is cooked it has a 'hollow' sound to it when you knock it.

SOYA PULP (OKARA)

The pulp left from making soya milk may be used in several ways. If the recipe does not include at least ½ hour cooking or baking, then the okara must be simmered for 30 minutes before it is used.

Okara may be added to any baking – breads, cakes, biscuits or pastries. It gives the food a slightly nutty, gritty texture you might like.

If you can think of nothing else to do with it, try your pets on it – my dog loves it!

Soysage

Take 2 cups of okara to 1 cup of wholewheat flour. Add 2 tbs tahini, 1 tbs yeast powder (autolysed), 1 tsp oregano, fennel, sage, savory, or any other herbs you like, and some kelp powder (if available). Taste as you go along until you get the flavour you want.

When ready put the mixture in a heatproof container covered with foil and place either in a pot of boiling water or in an oven at 130°C (250°F), gas mark ½, with a bowl of water in it. Cook for 1–1½ hours.

Eat as a savoury sausage.

Granola

Spread okara thinly on baking sheets and put in the oven to dry out (it takes an hour or more, so do this whilst baking other things).

Put in a wok, or large frying pan, with a dash of oil, some honey or malt extract, desiccated coconut, wheatgerm, sunflower and sesame seeds. Stir over a hot ring until things begin toasting and smelling good. Keep stirring or it will stick. Let it cool and put in an airtight jar.

Use with your breakfast, or with fruit salad, etc.

A WEEK'S MENUS

MONDAY

Breakfast:
Muesli with sesame seeds, buckwheat, wheatgerm, fresh peaches, apple juice.
Slices of wholemeal bread or toast.
Banana and tahini spread.
Peppermint tea.

Mid-morning:
Sliced apple.
Fresh fruit juice or herb tea.

Lunch:
Fresh carrot juice.
Beetroot, courgette, lettuce, mung bean sprouts, carrot and celery salad.
Wholemeal bread.
Orange and banana surprise.

Mid-afternoon:
Wholemeal bread with apple and almond spread. Cup of rose hip tea.

Dinner:
Savoury brown rice with chopped nuts.
Mixed salad of carrot, cauliflower, onion, radish.
Wholemeal bread.
Spinach soup.
Mixed fresh fruit salad.

Before bed:
Glass of fresh apple juice.

TUESDAY

Breakfast: Cooked buckwheat, millet and barley cereal with fresh orange juice.
Slices of wholemeal bread or toast.
Apple and nut spread.
Camomile tea.

Mid-morning: Banana.
Fresh carrot juice.

Lunch: Mixed bean sprouts, courgette and lettuce salad.
Wholemeal bread.
Lentil and onion soup.
Apple and grapefruit cocktail (fresh).

Mid-afternoon: Banana and tahini spread on wholemeal bread.
Cup of peppermint tea.

Dinner: Fresh celery and carrot juice.
Mixed lettuce, alfalfa sprout salad with fresh herbs.
Baked jacket potato.
Fresh grapes.

Before bed: Cup of rosemary tea.

WEDNESDAY

Breakfast: Muesli with a little goat's milk yoghourt and fresh pears and grapes.
Slices of wholemeal bread or toast.
Cup of fresh sage and lemon tea.

Mid-morning: Fresh celery juice (or celery and onion).

Lunch: Raw salad of lettuce, cabbage and chopped hazel nuts or sprouts, beetroot leaves, chives, mint.
Wholemeal bread.
Onion and carrot soup sprinkled with brewers' yeast.
Apricot and yoghourt fool.

Mid-afternoon:	Cup of rose hip tea. Slice of wholemeal bread with apple and apricot spread.
Dinner:	Large portion of brown rice salad, grated beetroot, chopped nuts and onion salad. Apple and wheatgerm surprise.
Before bed:	Cup of elderflower tea, with ½ tsp of honey. Add a little lemon juice to taste.

THURSDAY

Breakfast:	Cooked cereal with fresh orange and grapefruit. Wholemeal bread or toast with apple, almond and tahini spread. Mint tea.
Mid-morning:	Fresh fruit juice or herb tea. Apple.
Lunch:	Green salad. Leek and potato soup. Wholemeal bread. Fresh fruit.
Mid-afternoon:	Camomile tea (with lemon if liked). Banana.
Dinner:	Fresh celery juice. Large portion of coleslaw. Cooked brown rice with herbs, onion and nuts. Baked apple.
Before bed:	Lemon and thyme tea.

FRIDAY

Breakfast:	Muesli with a little goat's yoghourt and apple and orange (fresh). Slices of wholemeal bread or toast. Peppermint tea.

Mid-morning: Fresh carrot and orange juice.
Apple.

Lunch: Red cabbage and orange salad with chopped nuts.
Spiced vegetable soup with brewers' yeast.
Wholemeal bread.
Raspberry and yoghourt fool.

Mid-afternoon: Rose hip tea.
Pear.

Dinner: Celery, onion, lettuce and fresh herb salad.
Wholemeal bread.
Mixed bean stew.
Apple mousse.

Before bed: Lemon balm tea.

SATURDAY

Breakfast: Cooked cereal with fresh pears and grapes.
Wholemeal bread or toast with fruit and nut spread.
Rose hip tea.

Mid-morning: Fresh carrot and apple juice.

Lunch: Large portion green salad with chopped nuts.
Creamed onion soup.
Wholemeal bread.
Apricot and yoghourt fool.

Mid-afternoon: Camomile tea.
Banana.

Dinner: Fresh beetroot and lemon juice.
Brown rice pilaff.
Large portion of Spanish salad with sprouted seeds.
Apple and wheatgerm surprise.

Before bed: Cup of rosemary tea.

SUNDAY

Breakfast: Muesli with soaked dried apricots.
Apple juice.
Wholemeal bread with a little honey (½ tsp).
Mint tea.

Mid-morning: Fresh celery and apple juice.

Lunch: Baked vegetable casserole with tahini and coriander sauce.
Large portion of green salad with wholemeal bread.
Watercress (or lettuce) soup with wholemeal bread.
Fresh fruit.

Mid-afternoon: Cup of rose hip tea.

Dinner: Fresh carrot, parsley and apple juice.
Winter borscht with wholemeal bread.
Dandelion salad with humus.
Orange and banana surprise.

Before bed: Cup of peppermint tea.

APPENDIX 1

GOOD FOOD GUIDE

KEY:

****	Plenty
***	Moderation
**	Very little
*	Caution
●	None

agar-agar	***
alfalfa sprouts	****
almonds	****
aniseed – star anise	**
apple	***
apricot kernels	***
apricots – fresh, dried, wild	***
apricots – hunza	***
arame	**
arrowroot	**
artichokes – globe	**
artichokes – Jerusalem	***
asafoetida	**
asparagus	**
avocado	**
baked beans (soya – not tinned)	***
balanced salt	●
balm – lemon	**
banana	***
barleycup	*
basil – fresh or dried	**
bay leaves	***

bean sprouts .... ****
beans – aduki (cooked) .... ***
beans – aduki (sprouted) .... ****
beans – black-eyed .... ***
beans – butter .... ***
beans – dwarf French .... ****
beans – flageolet .... ***
beans – haricot .... ***
beans – kidney .... ***
beans – mung (sprouted) .... ****
beans – red .... ***
beans – runner .... ****
beans – soya .... ****
beer .... *
beetroot .... ****
blackberries .... **
blackcurrants .... **
borage .... ***
bread – brown .... ●
bread – rye (wholemeal) .... ***
bread – white .... ●
bread – wholemeal .... ***
broccoli .... ****
Brussels sprouts .... ****
buckwheat .... ***
buckwheat ramen .... **
buckwheat spaghetti .... **
bulgar wheat .... ***
butter – unsalted .... *
cabbage – red .... *
cabbage – white .... *
calabrese .... ****
cantaloup (melon) .... ***
cape gooseberry .... ***
cardamom .... **
carrot juice .... ****
carrots .... ***
cashews .... ***
cauliflower .... ****
celeriac .... **

celery .... *
cereals (only wholegrain) .... **
chamomile .... **
cheese .... •
cherries .... **
chick peas – dried .... ***
chickweed .... **
chicory .... ****
chilli .... •
Chinese cabbage .... ***
chives .... ***
cider vinegar .... **
cinnamon .... **
coconut – desiccated .... **
coffee .... •
comfrey leaves .... **
coriander .... **
corn – dried .... **
cornflour .... **
corn oil – cold-pressed .... *
corn on the cob .... ***
courgettes .... ***
couscous .... ***
cress – mustard and .... **
cress – water .... **
cucumber .... **
cummin seeds .... **
currants .... **
dandelion coffee .... *
dandelion leaves .... **
dates – fresh or dried .... **
dill .... **
eggs (after 3 months) .... **
endive .... ***
fennel .... ****
fenugreek – seeds or sprouts .... ****
figs – dried .... **
figs – fresh .... ***
fish (after 3 months) .... **
flour – wheatmeal .... •

flour – white	•
flour – wholegrain or wholewheat	***
fried food	•
fruit juices – bottled	•
fruit juices – canned	•
fruit juices – cartoned	•
fruit juices – fresh frozen	**
fruit juices – home-made	**
fruit juices – organically grown and bottled	**
fruit juices – sweetened	•
garlic	*
ghee (home-made only for cooking)	**
grapefruit	***
grapes	***
gravy powder	•
greengages	**
hazel nuts	***
hijiki	**
honey	**
hunza apricots	***
jams and preserves	•
jams and preserves – sugar free	*
kale	****
kelp	**
kidney beans – red	***
kiwi fruit	***
kohl rabi	****
kombu	**
leeks	****
lemon	**
lentils	***
lettuce – summer	****
lettuce – winter	**
loganberries	**
maize meal	**
mange tout (baby peas in pods)	***
margarines	•
marmite	•
marrow	***
melon – cantaloup	***

melon – honeydew .... ***
melon – water .... ***
milk (boiled only) .... *
milk – goat's (boiled only) .... *
milk – soya (boxed) .... **
millet .... ***
mint – fresh, dried .... ***
miso .... *
molasses .... *
muesli (not pre-packed) .... ****
mushrooms .... **
nectarines .... **
nutmeg .... **
nuts – almonds .... ****
nuts – brazils .... *
nuts – hazel .... ***
oats – rolled (not porridge oats) .... ****

oil – corn ⎫ all .... *
oil – olive ⎪ cold-pressed .... *
oil – safflower ⎬ for salad .... *
oil – sesame ⎪ dressing .... *
oil – sunflower ⎭ only .... **

okra .... *
olive oil .... *
olives – black .... *
olives – green .... *
onions .... *
onions – spring .... **
oranges .... ***
paprika .... **
parsley .... **
parsnips .... ●
pasta – white .... ●
pasta – wholegrain .... **
peaches .... **
peanuts .... *
peas – chick (cooked) .... ***
peas – garden .... ***
peas – sprouted .... ****
pepper – black, white .... *

peppers – chilli .... ●
peppers – red, green .... **
pickles (all kinds) .... ●
pineapple .... **
pistachios .... *
plums .... *
pomegranates .... *
potatoes .... *
potatoes – sweet .... ***
preserves and jams (sugar free) .... *
preserves and jams (with sugar) .... ●
prunes .... **
pumpkin .... ***
pumpkin seeds .... **
radishes .... ***
raisins .... **
raspberries .... **
rhubarb .... *
rice – brown .... ****
rice – white .... ●
rosemary .... **
ruthmol (salt substitute) .... **
rye bread .... ****
rye – flakes .... ****
safflower oil – cold-pressed .... *
sage .... **
salad burnet .... *
salsify .... ***
salt (balanced) .... ●
sea vegetables (e.g. arame, wakame, laverbread,
    dulse, kombu, hijiki etc.) .... **
seaweeds .... **
semolina – ordinary .... *
semolina – wholewheat .... ***
sesame oil – cold-pressed .... *
shallots .... **
shellfish .... ●
soya beans .... ****
soya flour .... ***
soya milk .... ***

spices .... **
spinach .... ***
spirits .... *
split peas .... ***
sprouted beans and seeds .... ****
squash – drink .... ●
squash – vegetable .... **
strawberries .... **
sugar (all types) .... ●
sulphur dried foods .... ●
sultanas .... **
sunflower oil – cold-pressed .... **
sunflower seeds – dry .... ***
sunflower seeds – sprouted .... ****
swedes .... ***
sweet potatoes .... ***
tahini (ground sesame seeds) .... **
tamari .... ●
tarragon .... **
tea .... ●
tea – herb .... **
thyme .... **
tofu .... **
tomatoes .... **
turmeric .... **
turnip .... ***
vegetable juices – home-made and organically
   grown .... ***
vegetable juices – organically grown
   and bottled .... **
vinegar – ordinary .... *
vinegar – cider .... **
wakame .... **
walnuts .... **
wheat berries .... ****
wheatgerm .... **
wine .... *
yeast extract – low salt .... *
yeast extract – other .... ●
yoghourt .... **

APPENDIX 2

THE RUDOLF BREUSS JUICE FAST

This juice fast is described in a book called *Cancer Leukaemia* by Rudolf Breuss, published by Rudolf Breuss Publishers, A-6700 Bludenz/Vbg Austria and distributed in the UK by Nuhelth, 9 Magdala Road, Nottingham NG3 5DE who also supply the herbs he recommends for the fast. The juice is available from Vessen Ltd, 320 London Road, Stockport, Cheshire.

Breuss, an Austrian herbalist and naturopath, claims he has treated about 2,000 people with cancer who have got well again by following his juice fast regime. He has many letters that support his claim.

Fasts cause the body to burn itself up in order to stay alive. European naturopaths and practitioners of Eastern systems of medicine have observed that the economy of the body is such that the diseased parts are used up faster than the healthy parts. Though this is not common knowledge in Britain the principles and practice of juice fasting are well established in Europe. In studies at the Karolynska Institute in Sweden it was found that route marches averaging 32.5 miles a day for ten days could be undertaken successfully while on a juice fast. The subjects experienced loss of weight, but felt vigorous and clear headed.*

For fasting, freshly prepared mixed vegetable and fruit juices are preferable to bottled juices. Their vegetable content is greater. When coming off a fast go gradually back to the Get Well Diet (Chapter 6). Start with small amounts of oatmeal

* *How to Keep Slim and Healthy with Juice Fasting*, Paavo Airola, Health Plus Publications, PO Box 22001, Phoenix, Arizona 85028, USA.

gruel and thin vegetable soup, then on to cooked cereal and honey followed by adding in mixed vegetable stews. After a few days of this gradually move on to the raw Get Well Diet.

An extract from *Cancer Leukaemia* with details of the Breuss Juice Fast follows by the kind permission of the publishers.

Important Teas for Cancer Treatment

1. Sage Tea

Put one or two teaspoons of sage in ½ litre of boiling water and boil for 3 minutes, then put it away. Sage contains a large amount of essential oils, which are very important for gargling, but for drinking it should not contain these oils therefore it has to be boiled for 3 minutes. After 3 minutes the oils are boiled away and at that moment the living enzymes are released, which are important for all the glands, spinal cord and the interarticular disc (meniscus). Because of this you should drink sage tea every day throughout your life. If you do, you will rarely suffer from illness.

When the sage tea has been boiled, put it away and you can still add St. John's Wort, mint, calmelite water etc. You then leave it to draw for 10 minutes.

2. Kidney Tea

My ingredients: Alpine Horsetail 15g, Nettles 10g (the best are picked in Spring). Bird knot grass 8g and St. John's Wort 6g. These quantities will last one person approximately three weeks. A pinch (holding between your thumb and two fingers) in a cup of hot water, leave to draw for 10 minutes, strain and once again add two cups of hot water and boil for 10 minutes, then strain and pour them together.

A question that many people ask is why kidney tea is prepared like this? Kidney tea contains five substances, which should not be boiled away. There is also a sixth substance (silicic acid) which we only get if it is cooked for 10 minutes.

Kidney Tea is only allowed to be taken for three weeks. It should be taken first thing in the morning before breakfast and before retiring to bed. Half a cup and drink cold. Last but not least discontinue drinking the Kidney Tea for a space of 2–3 weeks before continuing again. During this period do not have any meat broth, beef or pork.

3. Cranesbill Tea (Geranium Robertianum)
Every day drink one cupful cold. Add a pinch and leave to brew in hot water for 10 minutes.

Important References and Explanations

Sage Tea is the one I class as the most important of all the teas and should be drunk throughout your life.

Kidney Tea should be drunk for only three weeks, especially when suffering from inflammation and before operations. To prevent illness this Kidney Tea Treatment can be taken three or four times a year, but with intervals of at least two–three weeks.

By following my recipe exactly you will also cure any bladder problems.

Cranesbill Tea (Geranium Robertianum) is important for all the different cancers, especially if you have already had radium treatment, because it contains a small amount of radium.

My Total Cancer Treatment

Throughout this treatment you are not allowed to eat anything for 42 days, other than vegetable juices and the teas recommended only in the amounts stated. The juices can be drunk as much as required or until you are no longer hungry, though not more than ½ litre per day. (The less you drink the better.)

It is possible, and sometimes better, to make this juice yourself, especially if you have some knowledge of these vegetables biologically. If this is not the case or you do not want the trouble of making it yourself, a Swiss firm sells my 'Breuss Vegetable Juice' – made only from organically grown vegetables – to health shops and chemists.

My Juice Mixture: You take 3/5 beetroot, 1/5 carrots, 1/5

celery and add a little radish and an egg-sized potato, e.g. take 300g beetroot, 100g carrots and 100g celery and approximately 30g radish. It is not important to have the potato. Instead of the potato, you can also drink a cup of potato peel tea per day. Take a handful of potato peelings in 2 cupfuls of water and cook for 2 to 4 minutes. If the tea doesn't taste good then your stomach will not need it therefore you must not drink it. Press these various vegetables and put the juice through a tea sieve or a linen towel. For every ¼ litre of juice there will be a teaspoon of sediment – do not take this.

The cancer lives only from solid foods eaten by the humans. So if for 42 days you only drink vegetable juices and tea, the cancerous swelling dies.

You may during this time lose 5 to 15kg but you will feel well during this period. I myself have tried this treatment even though I didn't work during the course. It is better, if, a few days before starting this treatment, you drink approximately ¼ litre per day so that you get used to the juice. Drink it slowly with a spoon. Do not swallow it straight away. Every now and again you may have a mouthful of Sauerkraut juice if you wish.

APPENDIX 3

BEA VERNON'S STORY

Details of cancer

December 1975	Mastectomy, right breast. Clear until May 1977.
May 1977	Along scar – pink, then 'raucous' pink, then open sores. Lump on neck.
June 1977	Went on natural therapies: diet, relaxation, exercise, visualisation, healing, positive attitude, etc. Poultices on sores varied between comfrey, comfrey and red clover, slippery elm or pure honey, or cold water splashing. Cold water shower after hot water shower on rest of body, just to stimulate it.
By September 1977	Gradual improvement.
By December 1977	Much greater improvement. Many pure honey poultices (which I found a wonderful healer).
By March 1978	All sores cleared. Lump gone.
Until March 1979	Stayed on very strict diet as described below (i.e. for nearly two years). Wanted to 'make sure' and build health for the future.

From March 1979 until present

Widened diet somewhat, but still live on a really good 100 per cent whole food diet – three-quarters raw.

Am now retired, married again, lead an extremely busy, active and interesting life and still feel bubblingly well.

My return to health

Two and a half years after a mastectomy, I was faced with a dilemma. There I was with four open sores along my old scar and a lump on my neck – together with the knowledge that six people I knew well, all having had only orthodox treatment (i.e. operation, radiotherapy and chemotherapy), had all died within two years of their secondaries. (Not all people die in this time – but they had.)

What was I to do? I did not want to die. I wasn't at all afraid of death itself – but I wanted to live and I did not want to leave my children, who had already lost their father. There was no Bristol Cancer Help Centre; so I searched for books on alternative methods of treating cancer – and found them.

I got the 'message': we have billions and billions of cells in our bodies and every single cell in every single organ has a function to perform; and in order to do this efficiently, it needs to be well. To be well, it has to be fed properly. 'Whole balanced' food grows on the earth ready to feed these billions of cells. But, through no one person's fault, like fools, we set to and tamper with this food by adulterating, dyeing, depleting and 'chemicalising' it. Is it any wonder that we get unhealthy cancerous cells?

First, I went on the 'grape cure' – five weeks, then later six weeks on pounds and pounds of grapes daily. I felt very 'clean' at the end of that period, but the cancer was still there. I pondered hard and then realised that the grapes, although they must have cleansed my body beautifully, probably hadn't fed my cells enough to make all my organs work efficiently. So I changed tactics and decided to feed my body with masses of really good whole food.

But, another huge dilemma arose: different books said different things – 'Take oranges', 'Don't take oranges', 'Eat this', 'Don't eat this'.

Again I pondered hard and came to a big decision which helped me tremendously. Part of the philosophy of health is that one's body is a wonderful machine which should be helped to function properly; perhaps the best thing to do was to 'bombard' myself with a large variety of good whole food, covering all the essential minerals, vitamins, enzymes and so on, and let my body sort out what it needed.

Every book I read had said 'Don't worry'. So I completely stopped worrying about all the minor details – I just ate as much healthy food as I could find. But the books also spoke about being relaxed, calm, joyful, loving and positive in life. It was a Roman poet who said 'A sound mind in a sound body' and it became clear to me that as I felt healthier in body, so my mind and spirit found it easier to think and act more positively.

I plodded on with a grim determination (but not an ounce of tension or worry) to feed all my cells well – so that steadily more and more of my body was working 'mechanically correctly'. Gradually I felt better and better. Then I felt glowing, had more energy and could feel my body starting to work more efficiently.

After about six months, I reached the stage of feeling bubblingly well; and my sores and lumps started to diminish. I persevered and three months later they had gone.

To make sure that I was going to have healthy cells and so healthy organs in the future, I carried on strictly (but still not tensely) until two years had passed. I then just felt 'vibrant'. One has to experience this to know what it means. I felt much better than I did before I had cancer.

Now I am not quite so strict as during those two years and I have a wider diet at times – but I still live on a very healthy whole food diet with masses of salads and fruit. If someone offered me £100,000 to go back on an ordinary 'civilised' diet, I wouldn't do it because I feel *so* well! This is a pity – I could have given the £100,000 to the Bristol Cancer Help Centre!

The Diet

General rules
No salt, no sugar. I used only cold-pressed oil.
Everything was eaten raw except soups and beans, pulses and cooked nut dishes.
Red clover chewed a lot, or put into drinks.
I found that a food processor and a juice extractor were useful in coping with large amounts of vegetables.

Breakfast
Muesli (wheat, oats, rye, barley) plus sprinkled on top at least 2 of the following: sesame seeds, sunflower seeds, buckwheat, pumpkin seeds, linseed oil seeds.
Plus soaked dried fruit (2 of: dried apricots, sultanas, raisins, prunes, figs).
Plus fresh fruit.
Natural yoghourt on top.
2 slices of wholemeal bread and margarine and honey (*only* non-heated from non-sugar fed bees – obtainable direct from some beekeepers). Often used honeycomb also.
(*Note:* I used Flora margarine but would now use Vitaquell – a German brand.)

Mid-morning drink
One of the following:
Yerbama tea (Brazilian non-caffeine tea – obtainable from Yerbama Tea Co., Tavistock, Devon).
Vegetable stock
Pure fruit juice
Herb tea
Barleycup (no milk)
(*Note:* Red clover popped into drink also.)

Lunch
Huge salad, with everything I could lay my hands on, and with as much variety as possible of root and leaf vegetables.
Root vegetables:
Raw beetroot (with apple or other fruit)
Carrot

Onion
White turnip
Radish (red and white) .
Kohl rabi
Garlic
Leaf vegetables:
Lettuce (as fresh as possible)
Celery
Raw cauliflower
Raw sprouts
Bean sprouts (very important)
Red and white cabbage (not a lot)
Chives
Stalks from tree onions (green part)
Watercress
Garden cress
Green carrot tops
Chinese cabbage
Parsley
Dandelion leaves
Nasturtium leaves
Plus variety of herbs, including plenty of salad burnet, lemon balm, mint, etc.
Salad dressing: Cold-pressed oil and lemon or cider vinegar with yoghourt dressing, etc.
Plus nut, pulse, bean or millet dish, or cottage cheese. (Not too much as there is protein also in the vegetables.)
Dessert: fresh fruit.

Afternoon drink
As mid-morning.

Evening meal
Soup: using all outside leaves from salad, some root and leaf vegetables (especially curly kale), plus onions or leeks and garlic – as large a variety of vegetables as possible to provide a wide range of mineral salts. I also always used nettles, except when in flower – though you can usually find baby nettles tucked under those in flower. (Put on rubber gloves to pick

nettles, then hold stalk and strip off leaves.) I often added millet.

The family had potatoes in this soup and cheese on top, but I had only the odd small potato, or wholemeal bread, and no cheese.

Dessert: fresh fruit.

Evening drink
As mid-morning.

Bea Vernon, Sept 1983

PETE'S STORY

I have recently joined the team in the kitchen at the Bristol Cancer Help Centre. Twenty-four years old, I am 6 feet tall and, though a vegan, am as strong as an ox. It still surprises me that people assume a non-carnivorous diet is weakening.

About six years ago I began excluding meats and eggs from my diet and enjoyed the unfolding of new ideas, foods, tastes and attitudes that followed. Two years back dairy products began disappearing from my diet as I became more acquainted with the humble soya bean, and for the last 12 months I have not purchased any dairy products at all.

Having taken this step I feel in even better health; physically my resistance is higher and my catarrh problems are diminishing; mentally I feel more balanced, more aware and happier; spiritually I feel cleaner through not causing suffering to animals by eating and therefore killing them, and by not subjecting cows to lives of being milk producing machines. If you believe, as I do, that we are what we eat, then why should we expect that drinking the milk of a discontented cow will fill us with joy!

People often ask if it is expensive buying all the fresh and dried fruits, nuts and so on that make up a large part of my diet. My answer is that I have been feeding well on less than £8 a week for quite a while, and in fact this sum covers the buying of ordinary household goods.

My diet is still evolving. I'm now out of the habit of using salt automatically and it rarely finds its way into any of our meals. I'm slowly finding alternatives to sugar for baking and sweets, but with my tastes changing I want sweet foods less and less. I'm also coming to recognise the effects of carbohydrates on my body – usually a half-hour 'high' followed by a couple of hours sluggish thoughts and actions. The more pure and unrefined my eating becomes the more sensitive I am to the states of mind and body that foods put me in.

It is nice to see how amazed people are, when they first come across a vegan diet, at the tantalising tastes that can be created with a bit of effort and love. I'm still finding out how wide the field is.

GLOSSARY

Allopathy The Greeks called diseases allopathic, coming from outside the person, or homoeopathic, coming from within the person. Allopathy is a term used to distinguish modern Western medicine from other systems, since it began with the assumption that all disease is physical in origin, i.e. outside the person.

All trans see *Cis*

Cancer A disease characterised by uncontrolled growth of single types of cells which repel each other instead of keeping together. It is the result of a genetic change in cells which can be due to more than one cause.

Caponise From the French word *capon*, describing a cock whose sex organs have been removed, now used loosely for any castrated animal of either sex.

Carcinogen A substance that produces the genetic change found in cancer.

Cells Individual units of living matter, usually specialised for one function and having a controlling nucleus, an outer defining surface called a cell wall and a liquid content called cytoplasm.

Co-enzyme A compound which, though not itself an enzyme, assists an enzyme in its function(s).

Crustacea Animals with hard outer shells. They mostly live in the sea, some in fresh water and a few on land by the sea.

DNA Deoxyribonucleic acid is the main constituent of the genes (transmitters of hereditary factors) in humans. RNA (ribonucleic acid) is probably a precursor of DNA.

Duodenum A bulbous area at the top of the small intestine just below the exit of the stomach; the pancreatic juices and the bile empty into it.

Ecology The study of natural relationships between weather, soil, plants and animals.

Elements Single substances – compounds are made of more than one element.

Emulsion Oil and water do not mix. If shaken up briskly tiny bubbles of oil float evenly on the water. This can be facilitated by emulsifying agents. The formation of tiny bubbles of oil allows the solution of fat-soluble substances suspended in the water to go on faster by increasing the surface area of the oil.

Enzymes Compounds which bring about the transformation of one compound into another or others, without themselves being changed.

Epoxide Substances formed when PUFA take up oxygen and become rancid. They are unstable and can act as carcinogens (q.v.).

Fasting A total fast means going without food or water. A juice fast means having juices but no solid food. A dry fast means taking no water or juices and only dry solid food. Both are used medicinally.

Gastric Appertaining to the stomach. *Gaster* in Latin means stomach.

Homoeopathy Today this term is used to mean a system of therapy or medicine which employs, in very small doses, agents that give similar effects to the symptoms and signs of a disease, as opposed to allopathy (q.v.) which does the opposite.

Hydrocarbon A substance composed of hydrogen and carbon only, usually derived from mineral oil deposits.

Ions Electrically charged elements and compounds into which water-soluble compounds split up in solutions.

Ion-transporters These carry ions around the body. Proteins and compounds of phosphorus with fats do this but the term is usually applied to compounds manufactured from various acids which travel through the body fluids un-ionised and deliver their ions inside or on the cell wall.

Juice Fast see *Fasting*.

Kelp Common seaweeds of tidal shores in temperate climates, usually of the species *Fucus* and *Laminaria*.

Lactation The state of milk production.

Legumes Plants that grow pulses (q.v.).

Lymphatic System This is composed of open-ended fine tubules (lymphatics) lying in the tissue spaces outside the blood system which drain into lymphatic glands where the lymphatic white cells are generated. These glands drain by further lymphatics into the main vein of the body. About 30 gallons a day of tissue fluid are so drained off the tissues; otherwise we should be swollen bags of fluid.

Metabolism Chemical transformations that go on in bacteria, plants and animals.

Minerals A loose term meaning compounds, usually metallic, obtained from the soil.

Miso A fermented mixture of soya beans, salt and various grains. A good savoury, it contains vitamin B12, but is very high in salt.

Mitochondria Very small chemical factory units in the cytoplasm of cells (see *Cells*).

Molecule A single unit of a chemical compound – not an element (see *Elements* and *Ions*).

Mucoprotein A slimy protein secreted by mucous membranes, e.g. spit or phlegm.

Naturopathy A system of therapy based solely on changes of diet and life style. This therapy includes fasting, hot and cold packs, and baths. Sometimes spa therapy and herbs are required. It is mainly practised in central Europe.

Nutrient Something that nourishes as opposed to food consisting of empty calories that contain no nutrients, only energy. A word that applies to foods that have ample vitamins and minerals for their metabolism (see *Metabolism* and *Minerals*).

Orotic Acid An amino-acid that takes part in the energy-forming cycles of the body. It has the property of being an ion-transporter (q.v.) and readily forms salts (q.v.) with metals.

Pulses Peas, beans and lentils.

RNA see *DNA*.

Salt Salt is sodium chloride – a salt is a chemical compound formed by the union of a metal with an acid.

Shellfish An aquatic invertebrate with, usually, a hinged shell.

Valency An ability to form a chemical union. It can be single or multiple. A suitable prefix indicates the number of valencies an element or compound possesses.

Vegan A person who eats no animal products whatever.

SUGGESTED READING

Diet and Nutrition: a Wholistic Approach Rudolf Ballantyne MD (Himalayan International Institute, Hovesdale, Pennsylvania, USA, 1978)

Health on Your Plate Janette Pleshette (Hamlyn Paperbacks, 1983)

The Right Way to Eat Miriam Polunin (Dent, 1978)

The Cancer Prevention Diet Michio Kushi (St Michael's Press, New York and Thorsons, UK, 1983)

Food for Nought R. H. Hall (Vintage Books, Random House, New York, USA, 1974)

Cancer: Causes, Prevention and Treatment – the total approach Paavo O. Airola (Health Plus Publications, PO Box 22001, Phoenix, Arizona 85028, USA)

Mental and Elemental Nutrients Carl C. Pfeiffer PhD, MD (Keats Publishing Inc., New Caanan, Connecticut, USA, 1975)

ACKNOWLEDGEMENTS

Many people have helped to produce this book and I am deeply grateful for their efforts. Without them I could never have completed it in the time available and the circumstances existing in my life during those months.

S. Bhakta, Kathy Armstrong and Peter Davies provided delicious new recipes. Ute Brookman, Robert Armstrong and Edna Cook-Radmore also provided recipes and helped with the lay-out and editing.

Liza Dagnall, Eleanor Edgerley, Barbara Burt, Edna Cook-Radmore and Cynthia Slade did the typing.

Beryl Duncan Ray, Pat Pilkington and Cynthia Slade organised, deputised and generally kept things moving.

INDEX